# Socialism in Cuba

D0169597

# Socialism in Cuba

by Leo Huberman
and Paul M. Sweezy

Modern Reader Paperbacks
New York and London

Library of Congress Catalog Card Number: 68-8078
Standard Book Number: SBN-85345-133-8

First Modern Reader Paperback Edition 1970
First Printing

Published by Monthly Review Press
116 West 14th Street, New York, N.Y. 10011
33/37 Moreland Street, London, E.C. 1

Manufactured in the United States of America

*To the memory of Che*

*If . . . the choice were to be between Communism with all its chances, and the present state of society with all its sufferings and injustices; if the institution of private property necessarily carried with it as a consequence, that the produce of labour should be apportioned as we now see it, almost in inverse ratio to the labour—the largest portions to those who have never worked at all, the next largest to those whose work is almost nominal, and so on in a descending scale, the remuneration dwindling as the work grows harder and more disagreeable, until the most fatiguing and exhausting bodily labour cannot count with certainty on being able to earn even the necessaries of life; if this, or Communism, were the alternative, all the difficulties, great or small, of Communism would be but as dust in the balance.*

—John Stuart Mill,
*Principles of Political Economy*
(third and later editions)

# Preface

Brief titles cannot adequately describe the contents of a book, and *Socialism in Cuba* is no exception. It may therefore be helpful at the outset to tell the reader a little more about what this book tries to do.

There are certain problems that are common to all countries which have undergone a socialist revolution—that is to say, where the state power of the bourgeoisie and its domestic and foreign allies has been overthrown, a new government and army representing the interests of the exploited classes have been established, and all or most of the means of production have been transferred from the private to the public sector. Before the revolution, the basic structure and developmental tendencies of the economy and society were determined by international and domestic market forces. If this were to continue after the revolution, a more or less rapid reversion to the status quo ante would take place. But if the revolutionary government is serious about building a new society qualitatively different from the old, the economic structure and its mode of operating must be transformed to permit consciousness and will to take the place of the elemental socio-economic forces of the capitalist-imperialist system. This means that the revolutionary government must substitute itself for the market as the guide and engine of economic and social development. And this inevitably brings it face to face with a whole series of problems relating to its goals, the means for achieving them, and the obstacles which stand in the way. It is these problems as they have manifested themselves in Cuba, and what the revolutionary government has done to solve them, that constitute the subject matter of this book.

Countries containing about a third of the world's population have had socialist revolutions in the last half century, and there naturally exists a vast literature dealing with the way the problems which interest us here have arisen and been dealt with in various individual countries or groups of countries. But the comparable literature on Cuba, the youngest of the socialist countries, is still very limited both as to quantity and scope. Edward Boorstein's *The Economic Transformation of Cuba* is excellent, but it is largely restricted to the years 1960-1963 during which the author occupied responsible positions in the revolutionary government. Michel Gutelman's *L'agriculture socialisée à Cuba* is also of high quality and is based on three years of work and observation in the service of the revolutionary government, and the same can be said of I. Joshua's *Organisation et rapports de production dans une économie de transition (Cuba)*. But these two works by young French economists do not attempt to go beyond the agricultural economy. Our purpose has been the more ambitious one of dealing with both the whole revolutionary period and the whole economy, with attention in the last chapter to the interrelation of economics and politics.

We have of course drawn heavily on the works of Boorstein, Gutelman, and Joshua, as the reader will see, and we wish to express our thanks to these pioneering authors. Other debts to individual writers or books are duly noted in the footnotes. For the rest, we have relied on first-hand observation, discussions with dozens of Cuban and foreign experts, and study of available Cuban governmental and periodical publications. We visited Cuba twice in 1960, resulting in our earlier book *Cuba: Anatomy of a Revolution;* one of us returned in 1961 and 1965; and we were both in Cuba again in February and March of 1968. It would be a pleasure to name and personally thank the many people in and out of Cuba without whose help neither this book nor the earlier one could have been written. But we are aware that nearly everything in the book is controversial, and we fear that anyone we might name could be unfairly identified with opinions or conclusions for which, in the final analysis, we alone are responsible. So it seemed best to omit all credits except those which are explicitly recognized in the text and footnotes. Those who have been generous with their time and counsel will know to whom our thanks are addressed, and those who have most influenced our thinking will perhaps see something of their own ideas and convictions in what we have written.

For the second time in three years it is my sad responsibility to complete and sign the preface of a collaborative work alone. Leo Huberman died in Paris on November 9, 1968. But once again—as in the case of *Monopoly Capital* which I wrote together with Paul Baran—I can say that this in no way diminishes the joint character of the book. My partner left for Europe on October 23, and two days before his departure we spent several hours putting the final touches on nine of the eleven chapters. The other two were left with me for some further checking and rewriting. One of these I sent to Leo in London about a week after he left, and after making a few small editorial changes he okayed it. Only one chapter therefore had to be prepared for the printer after his death, and in that case everything except the final form had already been agreed on.

—Paul M. Sweezy

*New York City*
*January 1, 1969*
*Tenth Anniversary of the Cuban Revolution*

# Contents

# List of Tables

# Socialism in Cuba

# 1

# The Need for Socialism

Some nations in the world are poverty stricken because they lack natural resources. But that is not true of the Latin American countries. They have an abundance of the resources necessary to make a country rich. No continent in the world compares with Latin America in the amount of cultivable high-yield soil or in reserves of timber. List the metals important to industrial development—copper, tin, iron, silver, gold, zinc, lead—all of them and many others, as well as oil and hydroelectric power, are found in great abundance in Latin America.

Yet the people of Latin America are desperately poor. The statistics presented to Congress by the late President John F. Kennedy, in his message proposing the Alliance for Progress program on March 14, 1961, told the story:

The average per capita annual product is only $280, less than one-ninth of the United States—and in large areas, inhabited by millions of people, it is less than $70. . . .

The average American can expect to live 70 years, but life

17

expectancy in Latin America is only 46. . . . While our rate of infant mortality is less than 30 per thousand, it is less than 110 per thousand in Latin America. . . .

Illiteracy extends to almost half the adults, reaching 90 percent in one country. And approximately 50 percent of school-age children have no schools to attend. . . .

In one major Latin American capital a third of the total population is living in filthy and unbearable slums. In another country 80 percent of the entire population is housed in makeshift shacks and barracks. . . .

Poverty, illiteracy, hopelessness and a sense of injustice—the conditions which breed political and social unrest—are almost universal in the Latin American countryside.

Mr. Kennedy not only described the need, he also advised on the steps to be taken: "A program for improved land use, education, health, and housing. . . . There is an immediate need for higher and more diversified agricultural production, better distribution of wealth and income, and wider sharing in the process of development."

Mr. Kennedy's statement of the problem and the measures required to solve it were convincing, and the Congress of the United States adopted his Alliance for Progress aid program. Today, nearly eight years later, it has become apparent to almost everybody that the plan has one important defect—it won't work. Not because the appropriation isn't enough—it wouldn't work if the appropriation were multiplied ten times.

It won't work because it doesn't affect the imperialist relationship that is the fundamental cause of the conditions the United States says it wants to alleviate. Latin American countries are rich in natural resources, but their people are poor because their economies are lopsided; the wealth flowing from their natural resources is appropriated by U.S. monopoly corporations which have distorted these economies by their concentration on the extraction of profitable raw materials. The land that is not in the hands of foreign interests is held by

the native bourgeoisie—the traditional landowning aristocra-
cies now intertwined with the financial, commercial, and man-
ufacturing classes. Much of the land is out of cultivation and
much of the rest is underutilized. Unless and until the two
ruling groups—the foreign and domestic capitalists—are forced
to give up their power, property, and privilege, unless the
economic and social structure of these Latin American countries is radically altered, nothing fundamental will be changed.
The people will remain hungry.

The aid program won't do what Mr. Kennedy said it would
do because it does not give the Latin American countries
genuine independence; it does not break the economic stran-
glehold that U.S. imperialism has on the whole continent.
Without genuine independence, the Latin American countries
will remain, in effect, colonial appendages of the North American metropolis. And their most basic difficulties arise precisely from their past history and present status as colonial
appendages.

*But political independence, though of the utmost impor-
tance, is not enough; Latin American countries must win economic independence too.* And economic independence, in the
sense of establishing *their own control over their own economic surplus* so they can apply it to productive capital investment for the planned economic development of the whole
nation, involves those far-reaching social changes which spell
revolution—and socialism.

In the *New York Times Magazine* of Sunday, December 4,
1960, Senator Mike Mansfield addressed himself to "The
Basic Problem of Latin America." Here is what he proposed
must be done by any Latin American nation that wished to
develop:

(1) It must act, at once, to alleviate the most glaring inade-
quacies in diet, housing and health from which tens of millions of
people suffer.

(2) It must improve agriculture by diversifying crops, broadening land ownership, expanding cultivable acreage and introducing modern agricultural techniques on a wide scale in order to increase production, particularly of food.

(3) It must bring about the establishment of a steadily expanding range of industries.

(4) It must wipe out illiteracy within a few years and provide adequate facilities to educate an ever-increasing number of highly trained technicians, specialists, and professionals to provide the whole range of modern services.

(5) It must end the relative isolation of the beachheads from the interiors, and the parts of the interior from one another, by a vast enlargement of existing systems of transportation and communications.

Now, the interesting thing about this excellent prescription for curing the ills of the Latin American countries is that it was an age-old remedy prescribed by equally competent doctors years and years ago. In different words that said the same thing, it was prescribed for Cuba by the Foreign Policy Association in 1935, by the World Bank in 1950, and by the United States Department of Commerce in 1956. But the medicine was never swallowed—until the revolutionary government of Cuba came to power. Now, at long last, the things that needed doing, the measures for making Cuba a healthy instead of a sick nation, have been taken. What Senator Mansfield, and the Foreign Policy Association, and the World Bank, and the Department of Commerce, and President Kennedy said had to be done *is* being done—in *socialist* Cuba. But it is not being done, to any significant extent, in any of the capitalist, colonial countries of Latin America. Nor, we are suggesting, *can* it be done in those countries unless and until they too have their own socialist revolutions.

This is the lesson to be learned from the Cuban Revolution —a vitally important lesson for all Latin American countries.

The experience of Cuba proves beyond a doubt that a social revolution is an indispensable precondition for the initiation of economic growth and social development. The adoption of a planned economy is enabling Cuba to lay the groundwork for a balanced, healthy, educated, and eventually rich, society —a society in which the very nature of man himself may be transformed.

# 2

# Education

In his famous "History Will Absolve Me" speech at his trial, following the unsuccessful attempt of the revolutionaries to capture Fort Moncada on July 26, 1953, Fidel Castro spoke of six problems that "we would take immediate steps to resolve"—the problems of land, industrialization, housing, unemployment, education, and health. These, you will recall, were the same problems to which President Kennedy and Senator Mansfield addressed themselves.

The revolutionary regime took power on January 1, 1959. Immediately, it took the promised steps to resolve these problems. And nine years later, on February 11, 1968, a dispatch in the *New York Times* from Juan de Onis in Havana, indicated that progress continues to be made:

Cuba, under a revolutionary dictatorship, is pushing ahead its program harder and faster than most other Latin-American countries.

In mass education, public health, rural modernization, land use, economic diversification, administrative reforms and management of foreign exchange, Cuba has made important gains under Fidel Castro.

In education and in health Cuba's achievements have been especially notable. Nowhere else in the world—except possibly in the socialist countries of the Soviet Union and China—has so much been done in so short a time. Illiteracy in Cuba, as in underdeveloped countries everywhere, was highest in the rural areas. In 1960, Fidel explained the facts to the Cuban people and asked for a thousand men and women who had education beyond the level of second-year high school, to volunteer to go into the most remote areas of the country to teach reading and writing, hygiene, and nutrition. Five thousand people from all walks of life answered the call—including doctors and engineers who had to be dissuaded from going because the Revolution needed them in their own professions.

These volunteer teachers received special training in camps set up in the mountains; there was an average of fifty students per teacher—classes for youngsters were held in the daytime, for adults in the evening.

That was only the beginning. At the United Nations Assembly in September, 1960, Fidel Castro announced that on January 1, 1961, a great literacy campaign would be launched in his country. And so it was. The year 1961 was properly labeled The Year of Education and the entire population was mobilized to eradicate illiteracy. The Bay of Pigs invasion began on Saturday, April 15, and Fidel reported to the people on Sunday, April 23, after the counterrevolutionaries had been defeated, that one achievement of which the nation was justly proud was the fact that the anti-illiteracy program continued practically without letup during the entire invasion.

There had to be that kind of amazing devotion and discipline because the task which the revolutionary government had set for itself was stupendous: to rid the country of illiteracy *in one year*. Reflect on this for a moment—23.6 percent of the people, almost one in four, could not read and write. You can readily imagine how great a job it was just to cover the country, to search out where and who the illiterates were; then a veritable army had to be trained in how to teach; millions of books had to be printed for both pupils and teachers; then the teachers, ranging in age from ten to sixty, had to set up classes in schools, homes, stores, offices, and factories in the cities; or had to go to live in the most remote and isolated regions in the country to teach farmers and their families (ranging in age up to 106), many of whom had never before held a book in their hands.

The teaching force numbered 268,420. Of that number, 120,632 were "people's teachers"—adult volunteers who, inspired by the slogan "the people should teach the people," did their regular jobs and taught an average of two hours each day. Two of our friends were people's teachers: the wife taught a class of maids who worked in her neighborhood; the husband taught factory workers in the plant he headed.

The thirteen-year-old son of another friend was a *brigadista*, of whom there were some 100,000. When school closed a month early, in May, he was sent to a special school in Varadero for a two-week training course, then to a peasant's house in the mountains where he lived with the family until October, helping with the work and teaching. Girls, too, became *brigadistas* and taught in the rural areas, but they lived in groups, with a junior high school teacher in charge.

In September, when it became apparent that the student *brigadistas*—as well as their pupils—varied in ability, a call was sent out for reinforcements. It was answered by 13,016 workers who made up the Patria o Muerte Brigade, which promptly left for the rural areas to help the student *brigadistas*. The work in factories and offices that the Brigade members had to leave was made up by their comrades.

Then, finally, of a total of 36,000 school teachers, some 34,772 enlisted in the program to give the citizen *alfabetiza-dores* and the *brigadistas* the technical guidance they needed. So great was the task that the entire society had to be mobilized. In the press, at public meetings, in factories, offices, and on farms, the people were exhorted: "If you know, teach; if you don't know, learn." On the radio and TV came further prompting: "Every Cuban a teacher; every house a school." Mass organizations propagandized their members, poets wrote poems, artists painted pictures and designed posters, songwriters wrote songs, the press carried banner headlines on the progress made and ran photographs of participants in the campaign with letters from those who taught and those who were taught—the whole nation became involved in the great revolutionary cultural movement of eradicating illiteracy.

Some illiterates were ashamed and tried to hide the fact that they could not read or write; the aid of banks, post offices, and courthouses was enlisted to spot them, and then they were urged to participate. A million and a half copies of *Venceremos* [We Shall Conquer], the fifteen-lesson primer which includes photographs of Cuban life, were distributed. Each lesson was short and simple and those students who could read all fifteen, and who could then write a letter to Fidel, passed the final test and were entitled to receive a textbook with which to continue their study.

On the outskirts of Havana in a lovely small museum where the records, mementos, statistics, photographs, etc., of the literacy campaign are kept, we opened at random the book of letters to Fidel and came upon this one:

El Ingle, 14 June 1961

Dr. Fidel Castro
Prime Minister

I am making these few lines for you so as to tell you that I didn't know how to read or write and thanks to you, who put the literacy plan into practice, and to the teachers that are teaching me, I can already read and write. I am a *miliciano* and I work in the Rogelio Perea Cooperative and I would like you to come to this cooperative.

Viva la revolución socialista
Patria o Muerte
Venceremos

Yours truly,
Felix D. Pereira Hernández

Two tables, both taken from the 1965 United Nations Economic and Social Council (UNESCO) "Report on the Method and Means Utilized in Cuba to Eliminate Illiteracy,"[1] give the figures on those who learned how to read and write and those who did not:

Table 1
Total Number of Persons Taught
During the Literacy Campaign
(by provinces and by rural
or urban place of residence)

| Province | In towns | In the country | Total |
|---|---|---|---|
| Pinar del Río | 14,754 | 50,717 | 65,471 |
| Havana | 71,712 | 19,749 | 91,461 |
| Matanzas | 14,218 | 20,670 | 34,888 |
| Las Villas | 46,559 | 84,921 | 131,480 |
| Camagüey | 21,075 | 62,611 | 83,686 |
| Oriente | 62,739 | 237,487 | 300,226 |
| *Totals* | 231,057 | 476,155 | 707,212 |

[1] See p. 29.

At the end of the literacy campaign the illiterate population was:

## Table 2
### Total Number of Those Who Remained Illiterate (1961)
### (by provinces)

| Province | Population | Illiterates | Percent |
|---|---|---|---|
| Pinar del Río | 500,581 | 25,680 | 5.1 |
| Havana | 1,858,112 | 27,319 | 1.4 |
| Matanzas | 427,088 | 13,802 | 3.2 |
| Las Villas | 1,121,800 | 43,766 | 3.9 |
| Camagüey | 757,111 | 42,081 | 5.5 |
| Oriente | 2,268,561 | 119,347 | 5.2 |
| *Totals* | 6,933,253 | 271,995 | (avg.) 3.9 |

"The Campaign," says the UNESCO report,[2] "was not a miracle, but rather a difficult conquest obtained through work, technique and organization."

On December 22, 1961, the alphabetization program was officially ended—and illiteracy had plummeted from 23.6 percent when the campaign opened to only 3.9 percent when it closed. Never in the history of education anywhere in the world has there been so successful an achievement.

How great an achievement it was can be seen by comparing the 3.9 percent figure with those of the other Latin American countries, summarized in the Sixth Annual Report (1966) on *Socio-Economic Progress in Latin America:*[3]

According to the latest data supplied by the Latin American countries, about 33 percent of the inhabitants of the region are

[2] *Ibid.*, p. 72.
[3] Inter-American Development Bank (Washington: 1967), p. 31.

illiterate. . . . There are wide variations in illiteracy rates of the
Latin American countries ranging from 8.6 percent in Argentina
to 80 percent in Haiti. Between these extremes with a rate of
illiteracy that coincides with the regional median, is Ecuador,
where 32.5 percent of the population was illiterate in 1960.
Argentina, Chile, Costa Rica, Mexico, Panama, Paraguay, Uruguay, and Venezuela are above the median. The other countries
are below it.

The campaign against illiteracy in Cuba was just the opening gun in the battle. It was not a propaganda stunt to be
dropped when the point had been scored. It was the foundation for further spectacular successes in education. Many of
the workers and farmers who had learned to read and write
for the first time in their lives when a *brigadista* knocked at
their doors—instruction books and the Cuban flag in one hand,
and a paraffin lamp (the symbol of the campaign) in the other
—enrolled in the *Seguimento,* or follow-up classes, and continued their education. Today some of them are studying at
a university, others are managing enterprises in city and
country, and some are leaders in the government or the Party.

Even before the curtain had fallen on the end of the literacy
campaign, plans were already being made in the Ministry of
Education for a continuing educational program for workers
and peasants, with the necessary cooperation, as before, of the
trade unions, the Cuban Women's Federation (FMC), the
National Association of Small Farmers (ANAP), the Committees for the Defense of the Revolution (CDR), and other
mass organizations. To learn how to read and write—the attainment of a first-grade level—was not enough; the goal was
to bring the population of Cuba up to a sixth-grade level.

The first follow-up courses were started on February 24,
1962.

Prior to the Revolution, classes for adults had existed in
Havana and in a few of the larger cities but not in the coun-

tryside and the interior towns. These night schools were poorly attended both because workers in general were not motivated to attend and classrooms were not available for farmers, and because the teachers and materials used were the same as for children. When the Revolution came in 1959, in all of Cuba there were only 304 night schools with 1,369 teachers and some 27,956 students of whom only 50 percent were in regular attendance.[4]

In the six years since the Worker-Farmer Improvement Courses were instituted, one-half million adults, on the average, have been attending classes using materials and books (all free) suited to adults. Because of their maturity and experience, they progress much faster than children and more than one-third of a million have already won their sixth-grade diplomas. An unpublished report from the Ministry of Education, dated January 4, 1968, makes the picture clearer:

The efforts of one year of labor in Worker-Farmer Education can be illustrated with fundamental statistics: During 1966, for example, three calendars were developed with a total matriculation of 550,837 adults in urban, sugar, and mountainous zones, who studied in 30,756 classrooms with an average daily attendance of 66 percent. Instruction was carried out by 21,696 amateur teachers and 8,899 professionals, with total promotions of 258,154 in the five levels, of which 65,414 graduated from the sixth grade and 10,976 from the Secondary Course. The promotion of 60,622 adults, young in the immense majority, from the first level of the Primary Course, was a strong blow at residual illiteracy.

That record of accomplishment suggests some of the many difficulties encountered in this ambitious, massive program of making education available to the poor, to the workers and farmers whose cultural level in the past was so very low. Education for workers and farmers cannot be set up in the

---

[4] UNESCO report, *op. cit.*, p. 53.

traditional way with set hours in set places—teaching hours must be adjusted to fit the work schedule of the students, classrooms must be brought to remote rural areas where none existed before, and thousands of people must be hired as "teachers" who have never had a course in pedagogy. The "three calendars" in the "urban, sugar, and mountainous zones" are an illustration of the adaptation necessary to fit education to production: in the urban areas, classes are held from September to July; in the rural areas, classes must be held from June to December, the months when the work in the sugar crop has been completed; the January to October session in the mountainous areas is suited to the needs of the coffee crop.

In the rural areas, the classrooms for adults are those used by the children during the day. (Sometimes, because of work conditions, classes for adults are held at 5 A.M.!) In the cities, the classrooms are in the factories and offices. Flexibility in organization is essential; in both rural areas and cities, there may be places where there are not enough pupils to make up a class; and, because some of the older people who had willingly learned to read and write from a *brigadista* in their own home shy away from the idea of going to school and enrolling in a regular course, home reading circles are fostered in which the school goes to the home. Under the guidance of an amateur teacher, the residents of a specific area meet in a participant's home to improve their reading skills. Without such an effort, without an attempt to stimulate the habit of reading, there would undoubtedly be regression in the literacy rate and first-grade-level reading and writing would be, for many capable people, the end of their education instead of the starting point.

The words of the apostle José Martí, "To know how to read is to know how to walk," are frequently heard over the special radio and TV programs designed for workers and peasants.

In addition, 50,000 copies of the magazine *El Placer de Leer* [The Joy of Reading], especially suited to new readers, with national and international news in easy-to-read language, are distributed free of charge. To make the habit of reading a necessity—and a pleasure—to hundreds of thousands of culturally deprived workers and farmers to whom even newspapers, let alone books, were hitherto unfamiliar is a difficult struggle.

Fortunately, the Ministry of Education is well aware of the immensity of the problem. This became clear in a conversation we had with Raúl Ferrer, Director of Worker-Farmer Education, who told us:

Our teaching staff is, in great measure, not qualified at this time. They are being prepared in special pedagogical institutes, but of 30,000 teachers only about 8,000 now attend teacher-training schools. At the present moment we have 26 seminars teaching 5,000 future teachers.

This department is the university of adult education. We must derive, from our own experience, the system by which illiteracy can be abolished and the cultural level raised. One law we have learned—that there is no education of the masses without the direct participation of the organizations to which the masses belong.

Industrial workers, farmers, ranch workers, women, youngsters, all need special handling and we cannot apply the books and methods of one to the other. We are constantly adapting our programs to meet reality. We face real obstacles: there are no manuals, we have been compelled to revise wrong practices, but we have been able to go forward because we are always critical of our work.

We want every worker to be a student, and every student to be a worker.

The "battle of the sixth grade" was won in 1966 by 65,414 workers and peasants; and 10,976 graduated from the secondary course. This latter group is now eligible for higher education in the industrial and agricultural technology institutes, and in the Worker-Farmer Faculty of the three universities in Havana, Santa Clara, and Santiago. (How many workers and farmers had an opportunity in pre-revolutionary Cuba—or have the opportunity in the Latin American countries today—to attend a university, at no cost, with books and board and room paid for?) José Nazario González, Rector of Santa Clara University, told us that of the 5,000 students there in March, 1968, some 1,300 were workers and farmers.

Education is open to workers not only in schools, institutes, and universities, but in the factories themselves. This we learned from Juan Ramírez Leiva, a molder at the nickel plant in Nicaro. Juan entered the plant as a day laborer in 1963, when he was twenty-four. He had had only a third-grade education. In 1964 he enrolled in a one-year course in the general foundations of technology given in the plant at night; he worked eight hours, then studied two hours every night. Next he enrolled, with twenty-three other workers in the plant, in a six-month course in molding and the problems of casting metals. On the completion of that course, he took a one-year course in theory. This time he worked six hours each day and studied four hours, five days a week. Then, having finished the courses in both practice and theory, he became a molder. As a day laborer his wages had been $5.24 per day; as a molder, he gets $8.40 per day.

He told us: "I had to do a job of military work in the mountains, so I lost a year of study. Of course, I plan to go back to studying now. I was a member of the Young Communists and now I am a member of the Party. I like Party work but I prefer the work in the factory. Of the other eleven members of my last class, four are members of the Party, the others are not."

Juan is not a special case at Nicaro; 70 percent of the

workers there are enrolled in study classes taught by the technicians in the plant. And in the other nickel plant, at nearby Moa Bay, the University of Oriente has part of its School of Mechanical Engineering, with the plant engineers doubling as professors. Many of the workers there, like Juan at Nicaro, are studying under these professors and some will become engineers. Work and study have been merged. And it works the other way around too—students become workers, just as Raúl Ferrer hoped: at the University of Oriente some students spend their fifth year, their last, in rotating in different industries, including the nickel plants at Nicaro and Moa.

The magnificent effort to supply educational opportunities to the adult population of socialist Cuba is matched by the achievements in education for children. Before the Revolution the picture of primary-school education in Cuba was like that in most Latin American countries—deficient in both quantity and quality: not enough schools, particularly in the countryside; not enough teachers and not enough good teaching; not enough books and materials; too much graft which channeled the money supposed to go to education into the pockets of higher-ups in government. In short, it was a picture which made for a very high rate of illiteracy and ignorance.

The Revolution brought an immediate, spectacular change in quantity, if not in quality; in attitude toward education for the masses; and in willingness to allocate the funds necessary to make the desired improvements. One set of figures proves the point in respect to quantity:

In 1958 about 737,000 Cuban children, less than two-thirds the number aged seven through fourteen, were attending public or private primary schools in all grades up to the sixth. Because some of those who did attend were outside the normal age limits, the actual proportion of children between seven and fourteen in school was nearer five out of ten. In 1962, four years later, primary enrollments were estimated to be 1,350,000, and about eight in every ten Cubans aged seven through fourteen were enrolled.[5]

From an enrollment of only 50 percent of all children between seven and fourteen, to 80 percent in just four years! What so great an increase in the number of children being educated means in terms of the construction of additional school buildings, the printing of new textbooks and other learning materials, and the training of teachers can readily be imagined. In teaching, as in the other professions, there had been an exodus to Miami of thousands of the best-trained people. How is Cuba meeting the problem of training the veritable army of new teachers necessary for so great an expansion in education?

The contrast with the United States is striking. In our affluent, consumption-oriented society, childhood, especially in the middle and rich classes, can be a prolonged, easygoing period with a minimum of responsibility. Not so in Cuba where the lack of trained manpower—the hallmark of under-development—necessitates the enrollment of the whole population, including the children, in the spirited struggle to construct a new society.

The training of primary-school teachers in Cuba begins with the completion of the sixth grade. The students spend the next five years in boarding schools where life is rugged, work is hard and disciplined. It is that way by design—the theory being that most of the teachers in training will, at some time or other, be assigned to classrooms in the country-side and in the mountains and this conditioning in their

---

[5] Dudley Seers (ed.), *Cuba, The Economic and Social Revolution* (Chapel Hill: University of North Carolina Press, 1964), pp. 223-224. The five chapters on education by Richard Jolly are very detailed and informative.

period of training will better equip them for the primitive life to come.

The first link in the chain is the one-year course at the school at Minas del Frío, on a mountaintop in the Sierra Maestra in Oriente. The subjects taught are mathematics, history, geography, biology, Spanish, and physical education.[6]

The next stage is a two-year course on another mountaintop, the Manuel Ascunce Domenech School at Topes de Collantes in the Escambray mountains in the province of Las Villas. The subjects of study in the first year at Topes are the same as at Minas del Frío except that biology is here centered on animals instead of on plants. In the second year, the last at Topes, three new subjects are added: physics, drawing, and pedagogy.

We were taken by jeep to the school at Topes (Minas, too, is accessible only by jeep or on foot) and had the opportunity of seeing some of the classes there, of talking to the students and teachers, and, under the guidance of Manuel Rua Rodríguez, the director, and his assistant Carmen Hernández, we got a view of the whole school area and its functioning. The school has long outgrown the large initial building which was formerly a luxurious private tuberculosis sanitarium. To accommodate the 7,100 students, 402 teachers, 407 administrative and service workers, and 300 construction workers, many new buildings, dormitories, playing fields, and houses have had to be built. This university-like setting on a mountaintop has to have its own water and electricity systems. A large open-air amphitheater seating

---

[6] In a speech reported in *Granma*, August 18, 1968, Minister of Education José Llanusa Gobel reported that in the future Minas del Frío would admit "only students from the province of Oriente. In the other provinces there will be other provincial schools, also located in the rural areas, preferably in the mountains." The second and third steps in the teacher-training program will remain the same.

the entire school population where movies are shown on Saturday night, always preceded by a science short or documentary, was built recently—one of many projects included in the $1,800,000 allocated last year for new construction.

The school day is long, from 6:30 A.M. to 10:30 P.M. Evening hours are divided between homework, social activities, and taking care of personal needs. The students service themselves—they do their own laundry, make their own beds, clean up their too-crowded dormitories, wait on table in different shifts and, in the daytime hours, also help in all phases of construction work. Sundays are free, usually reserved for sport activities and picnicking on the lovely grounds with relatives and friends.

The teachers are even busier than the students. Most of them are themselves graduates of Topes who are continuing their own education in classes given at the school on Saturday nights by professors from Santa Clara University.

In our spontaneous, completely private talks with the girls and boys in their separate dormitories, we had an extended discussion with Oscar Rivero, a bright-eyed black lad from Havana. He had enrolled at Minas del Frío in 1966 when he was fifteen. Because as a youngster he had had to help his father, he had fallen behind in his studies. When he finally had the chance to make up his studies and pass the sixth-grade qualification test, he was two years older than the normal age for entrance into Minas del Frío. (Because educational opportunity was offered to them for the first time only after the Revolution, many students in the teacher-training program are, like Oscar, considerably older than will be the case in the years to come.) Oscar liked Minas better than Topes because there "conditions were more related to nature —we were outdoors much more of the time."

"Are you homesick?" we asked.

"Not particularly. My mother is happy now that I am studying hard."

"What does she do?"

"She works in a children's nursery."

"What subject do you like best?"

"Math is my favorite—though I really like football best, and productive work out of doors. I do my homework from half-past eight to half-past ten at night."

"Are you a Communist?"

"Not yet, but I hope to become a Young Communist this year."

"Why?"

"Because the Young Communists are the ones who induce others to work and make our country go forward."

"Are all the students here enthusiastic about the Revolution?"

"I hope so. But this cannot be fully determined because who knows what everybody thinks?"

"We have met some people who tell us that Cuba was a better country before the Revolution. What's your answer to that?"

"It's not true. Cuba is better now in everything. For example, today the government enables young people to study, gives more and better work to workers, creates workers' clubs, nurseries, and in general gives people better conditions not existing before."

"Do you believe that, or did you read it somewhere?"

"I see it."

"In what way?"

"Had there been no Revolution many of the opportunities we have today would not be available. I would have studied when I was younger, but I didn't have the chance, I had to help my father. My family lives better in every way than before the Revolution. They used to tell me of the troubles they had—lack of work, hunger, a whole series of problems. Now they are not hungry. All are working or studying."

The Makarenko Pedagogical Institute at Tarará just outside of Havana is the final stage in the training of primary-school teachers. Graduates of Topes, having completed their eighth and ninth grade courses, come to Makarenko for two more years of study and practice teaching. They study mathematics, history, geography, science, a foreign language, political economy, psychology, physical education, and pedagogy. They teach 60,000 children in 250 schools in Havana Province by day (the tenth-grade students teach in grades one to four, and the eleventh-grade students in grades five and six), and they study at night. This is the schedule of these youngsters filling a responsible adult role:

6 A.M.: Get up
6:30 A.M.: Breakfast
7 A.M.: Bus to Havana
8 A.M.: Teach until noon
12–2:30 P.M.: Bus back, lunch, and rest
2:30 P.M.–5 P.M.: Study
5 P.M.–6 P.M.: Physical Education
6 P.M.–8:30 P.M.: Bath and dinner
8:30 P.M.–11 P.M.: Classes

Saturday morning: Prepare classes for the next week
Saturday afternoon: Free
Sunday 6 A.M.–11 P.M.: Free

When we suggested to some of the Makarenko authorities that this seemed too heavy a schedule for a long-term period, we were told that time was of the essence, that these students were "soldiers in the army of education." That, indeed, was the attitude of the Makarenko students themselves.

This, then, is the track for those who are in training to become primary-school teachers. Would-be secondary and pre-university teachers take a different course. After nine years of study (i.e., after completion of what would be junior high school in the United States), they can attend a five-year course at a pedagogical institute. At Santa Clara University they study at the university their first year, spend the second year practice teaching, the third at the university, the fourth practice teaching, and the fifth at the university.

We attended classes at every educational level, some taught by graduates of Makarenko, and some by teachers who had been trained prior to the Revolution. One memorable experience we had was in a large new housing development in a slum area of Santiago where we visited a school with the unforgettable name, Dawn of the 26th of July Nursing School.

Because we might be carriers of germs, we were not permitted to enter the first classroom, but we could look through the screened windows. We saw eleven children, ranging in age from forty-five days to eighteen months, attended by three teachers all wearing gauze masks over nose and mouth.

The second classroom had twenty-three children ranging in age from eighteen months to four-and-a-half years, attended by five teachers. They were having a snack. Though such small children are generally delightful, we were especially thrilled because we saw there what was to become a commonplace in all other classrooms we visited later—black and white children together everywhere, complete integration. The new generation in Cuba will be completely free of racial prejudice.

The director of the school told us that the school had been open only a few weeks. Though there were only thirty-four children at this time—because the housing development was not yet completely finished—the school has a capacity of one hundred, with one teacher for every five children, apart from kitchen and cleaning help, etc. The building was impressive, very clean, with magnificent equipment, showers, sinks, all spic and span. There will be a nurse in attendance from 6:30 A.M. to 6:30 P.M. each day and a doctor will come to the school three times a week, and more when necessary. As we were saying goodbye, two Public Health inspectors arrived.

They come to the school each week to check on the hygienic conditions, to test the food, and to make sure that all health standards are being met.

The growing number of such nursery schools makes it possible for mothers to take jobs and to study. With the children so well taken care of—meals and school clothing are provided free of charge—the women of Cuba are in a position to free themselves, to participate as equals with men in useful work, and to raise their level of education and culture. The Cuban Women's Federation is very active on this front, working with the Worker-Farmer Education Department to end the inferior status of women.

Some women serve as technician-guides in the remarkable program of Interest Groups, or "circles for the promotion of interest in scientific and technical matters." These groups consist of students from the fourth grade up to the age of fifteen who meet several times a month, in out-of-school hours, to pursue a particular hobby. Some 178,000 children participated last year in 13,956 circles at the primary level, and 2,934 at the middle level. We went to an exhibition of their work in Havana and were amazed at the extent of their knowledge in the various fields they had been studying: the growth of sugar cane, coffee, citrus trees; how to make the special brand of Coppelia ice cream (fifty-four varieties of the best ice cream we have ever eaten!); the fishing industry; clouds and rain (a scientific explanation by a fifteen-year-old was completely over our heads); and a number of other scientific and technical subjects. The ten-year-old boy who lectured on coffee, with maps on a board and pointer in hand, was so knowledgeable that we were convinced he had memorized his speech; we stopped him in the middle and asked questions —he hadn't memorized it, he *knew* the subject. After a tour of the various stands with groups of youngsters clutching at our coats eager to explain, we left the room very depressed—they knew so much and we were so ignorant!

When we left we took with us a picture of Che with a letter to his nine-year-old daughter, a present from the Che Guevara Interest Group. This is the letter, written during the time of his disappearance, prior to his departure for Bolivia.

February 15

Hildita dearest,

Although this letter will reach you late, I am writing today because I want you to know I am thinking of you and hoping that you are enjoying a very happy birthday.

You are a big girl now and I cannot write you childish nonsense or little white lies. As you know, I am far away and can't come back to you for a long time, because I am doing what I can in the struggle against our enemies. What I am doing isn't much but it's something, and I think you can be proud of your father, as I am of you.

Remember that we face many years of struggle, and even when you become a woman you will have to do your part in the struggle. Meanwhile, you must prepare yourself. To be a good revolutionary at your age means to learn—as much as you possibly can—and to be ready always to defend just causes. Also, you should obey your mother. You mustn't think you know all the answers yet; you are still learning.

Try to excel as a student; excel in every sense, and you know what that means. It means study and a revolutionary attitude. In other words: good conduct, responsibility, love for the revolution, a fraternal attitude toward your school comrades, etc.

That wasn't how I was at your age, but I lived in a different society, where man was the enemy of man. But you have the privilege of living in another epoch and you must be worthy of it.

Don't forget to keep an eye on the other kids at home and tell them to study and behave themselves—especially Aleidita, who pays attention to what you say because you're her big sister.

Well, darling, once more I wish you a happy birthday. A hug for your mother and your cousin, and for you a big strong hug— to last for all the time we won't see each other—

from your

Papa

Another important aspect of the program of education is the School Goes to the Countryside plan in which some 300,000 students and teachers, from secondary-school level up, move to the countryside for six weeks to do productive work in agriculture and livestock raising. It is camp living and hard work, combined with some hours of study, TV educational programs, sports, and recreation. We saw two groups of secondary school *becados* (scholarship students), one leaving and the other coming to the fairly primitive tent camp site to do their bit in the gigantic coffee-planting project in the Havana Green Belt. We talked as we ate the much-too-starchy lunch of beans, rice, potatoes, rolls, yogurt, and cake. We asked one boy what he would do on completion of his school work and his reply was fairly typical: "I am going to be a doctor, but if the Revolution needs me somewhere else, I'll do that." We call this typical because in answer to a similar question put to Oscar Rivero and other students at Topes and Makarenko we got similar answers. We asked: "After you graduate, will you teach in Havana or in the country?" Always the same answer: "I will teach in the country districts, but I will go where the Revolution needs me."

This is a reflection of an outstanding feature of the education program in Cuba: its concentration on bringing education to the most remote areas, places where there had been few or no schools, places where illiteracy was greatest. Many of the 250,000 *becados* who receive housing, food, clothes, transportation, books—all free—plus a small monthly stipend, are boys and girls from the country.

*Becados* live in boarding schools (some of the most luxurious houses and apartments of rich refugees are now their living quarters) and get three meals a day plus a snack; but day-school children also get a snack and one or two meals—all free.

Textbooks, too, millions of them—five million in 1967, to be exact—are free to all students. The claim is made that whereas only one million books of all kinds were published in Cuba before the Revolution, eight million books were published in 1967 alone. For the Book Institute, in charge of book publication in Cuba since 1967, a book is no longer a commodity but a social necessity. For that reason and because the technological progress of the advanced countries has been, in part, made possible by the exploitation of the underdeveloped countries—Philosophy Professor Rolando Rodríguez, head of the Book Institute, explained to us—Cuba feels it has the right to disregard copyright conventions and publish whatever books it finds useful from any country in the world. Accordingly, it has reprinted, without payment of royalties, over 1,300,000 copies of the best work of authors everywhere, particularly in the fields of science and technology, and has made them available to its advanced students, scientists, technicians, and teachers.

This is, of course, of special importance to the students on the highest rungs of the Cuban education ladder, the thousands in the many technological institutes, and the 34,500 in the three universities which, of necessity, have changed their emphasis from the humanities to science and technology. The necessity is obvious: an economy determined to move from underdevelopment to development has immediate need for engineers, mechanics, electricians, chemists, agronomists, technicians, administrators—not for lawyers. As a result, two hundred students are in the Law School today; before the Revolution, there were six thousand. What are those students

who might have gone into law studying now? President
Dorticós gave one answer when he made the statement that
"2,000 engineers will graduate in Cuba in the period 1967-
1970. This figure is greater than the total number of engineers
graduated between the time of the establishment of the
Republic and 1959."[7]

As much a handicap as the shortage of skilled technicians
and administrators is the lack of a scientific tradition. Now a
beginning is being made. A listing of the various faculties at
Santa Clara University, each awarding a Bachelor's Degree
(the equivalent of a Master's in the United States) after five
years of study, shows where the emphasis lies in Cuban
university education today:

> Faculty of Agricultural Sciences: two schools
>> Agronomical Engineering
>> Veterinary Medicine
>
> Faculty of Technology: four schools
>> Mechanical Engineering
>> Electrical Engineering
>> Chemical Engineering
>> Industrial Engineering
>
> Faculty of Sciences: three schools
>> Psychology
>> Mathematics
>> Chemistry
>
> Faculty of Humanities: two schools
>> Public Accounting (Administration)
>> School of Letters
>
> Faculty of Medicine: six-year course,
>> the last year in internship

---

[7] *Cuba: Man, Revolution* (Havana: n.d.; in English), pp. 12-13.

Both university students and those in schools of industrial and agricultural technology have their military training while at school; and the work and study program, the union of physical and intellectual work, holds for them too, when the university is closed for forty-five days while professors and students cut cane.

Many of the best-trained people with advanced technical skills who fled the country after the Revolution are now being replaced by graduates from universities and technological institutes. There are not nearly enough to fill the need, but progress is being made and this kind of story is becoming increasingly common in the columns of Cuban newspapers:

### 123 TECHNICIANS FOR FERTILIZER PLANTS GRADUATE SUNDAY FROM ERNST THAELMANN TECHNOLOGICAL SCHOOL

At 3:00 P.M. next Sunday at the Ernst Thaelmann Technological-Industrial School, 123 students will graduate. They will work as technicians in mounting [setting up] fertilizer plants. This is the second graduating class of specialists in this branch of technology.

The above-mentioned school offers eleven specialties including that of plant operator, pump mechanic, electrician, turner, milling-machine operator, solderer, and others.

The 123 graduates were distributed by specialty as follows: 14 maintenance electricians, 12 turners, 12 milling-machine operators, and 85 evaporator mechanics.

This graduation is of great importance for carrying out the tasks involved in the development of the national economy, inasmuch as the technical cadres who have just been trained will work in the supervision and operation of fertilizer plants now being set up in our country.[8]

As fast as they pour out of the technological institutes, these

8 *Granma*, March 1, 1968.

newly trained Cuban youngsters replace the Soviet, Czech, and German technicians and specialists from the other socialist countries who taught them in school, factory, and farm. We made a spot check on the quality of their training by asking the directors of the nickel plants in Nicaro and Moa, the bulk sugar terminal in the port of Cienfuegos, and the Institute of Animal Husbandry near Havana whether any graduates of the special technical schools had been added to the staff. In every case they answered yes—the numbers hired varied from twelve to twenty-one, young people eighteen to twenty-four—and in every case their training and work were commended by their superiors.

Perhaps the most spectacular instance of Cuban technicians learning to fill the skilled manpower needs of their economy is the Moa Bay nickel plant where, the *New York Times* reported on February 5, 1968, "production is going up each year here thanks to considerable ingenuity in the training of technical personnel."

José Alemany, the twenty-nine-year-old engineer in charge of the plant, was in his last year of electrical engineering at Louisiana State University when he returned to Cuba in 1961. All of the engineers on his staff have received their training in Cuba since the Revolution. The plant they are running was designed and constructed by the Freeport Sulphur Company of Louisiana just before the revolutionaries took power. It was the most advanced of its kind in the world. "Freeport Sulphur," Mr. Alemany told us, "should be proud of having built such a plant, and the Cubans should be proud of being able to run it."

After our tour of the plant that has for the last three years won the award as the most efficient state industry in Cuba, we agreed. So, too, did the reporter for the *New York Times*[9] who wrote a long account in which he was impressed by the ability

[9] *New York Times*, February 5, 1968.

of the Cubans to maintain the highly delicate machinery in good condition:

In the machine shop, Cuban welders delicately soldered a seam on a titanium heat exchanger that is essential to the process. Titanium, which costs $25,000 a ton, calls for very advanced metallurgy, which the Cubans have learned with experience under Soviet instructors.

"These heat exchangers are worth $40,000 each, and they used to be sent to the United States for repairs at $10,000 a crack. We do the work here now," said Mr. Alemany.

What began as a matter of principle for the revolutionary government—that it is unjust and morally wrong for education to be denied to all the people, that the first step in creating the new man in a socialist society is to raise his cultural level —has turned out, in practice, to be the key to the problem of revolutionizing Cuba. Education of all the people is seen as the foundation for the development of the individual, and this in turn increases his usefulness to society and thus makes for the development of the country. The mobilization of the human resources is the touchstone for the mobilization of the economic resources.

So today, eight years after the end of the literacy campaign, Cuba is still a nation at school. The statistics shout the story— they are here in Table 3, as reported to the people by Fidel in his speech of March 13.[10]

The population of Cuba is estimated at eight million. This means that 27.6 percent of the people in Cuba are now getting some form of organized instruction. How very impressive this total is can be gauged by making two comparisons. The first, before and after the Revolution: in 1957, the latest pre-revolutionary year for which reliable figures are available, the population of Cuba was 6.4 million and school enrollment

10 *Granma*, March 24, 1968.

Table 3
Education

|  | Students |
| --- | --- |
| Primary school | 1,391,478 |
| Junior high | 160,308 |
| Pre-university (senior high) | 16,779 |
| Technical and professional training | 45,612 |
| Primary school teachers' training | 18,121 |
| Universities | 34,532 |
| Adult education | 405,612 |
| Others | 7,092 |
| Workers' technological institutes | 46,595 |
| Agricultural and stockraising schools for young people | 28,832 |
| Construction workshop schools | 10,663 |
| Military technological institute | 1,626 |
| Ministry of Public Health | 6,060 |
| School of higher physical education and sports | 2,462 |
| Day nurseries | 33,662 |
| *Total* | 2,209,434 |

was about 819,000, or roughly 12.8 percent; in 1968, with the population of Cuba having increased 25 percent, the number getting some form of organized education has gone up almost 170 percent!

The second comparison is with the other countries of Latin America. Not one of them comes near the Cuban enrollment in schools, and for all the countries as a whole, the figure is 16.8 percent compared to Cuba's 27.6 percent. Here are the statistics, from a table in the Report of the Inter-American Development Bank, previously cited:[11]

[11] *Op cit.*, p. 37. The table gives enrollment at "primary, intermediate, and higher levels" only. It may be that adult education figures are not included, but since in none of these countries is that of great importance, the comparison is basically valid.

Table 4
Total School Enrollment as a
Percentage of Total Population

| Country | Total |
| --- | --- |
| Argentina | 19.4 |
| Bolivia | 15.7 |
| Brazil | 15.0 |
| Chile | 20.7 |
| Colombia | 15.8 |
| Costa Rica | 22.6 |
| Dominican Republic | 16.0 |
| Ecuador | 17.2 |
| El Salvador | 15.3 |
| Guatemala | 10.5 |
| Haiti | 6.5 |
| Honduras | 13.4 |
| Mexico | 18.6 |
| Nicaragua | 14.5 |
| Panama | 21.6 |
| Paraguay | 20.4 |
| Peru | 20.3 |
| Uruguay | 18.5 |
| Venezuela | 19.7 |
| *Latin America* | 16.8 |
| *Cuba* | 27.6 |

We are not suggesting for one moment that the quality of Cuban education is as impressive as the quantity. It is not. It was obvious in the classes we attended at all levels that some of the teachers are poorly trained and that much remains to be done in the field of pedagogy. But it is also obvious from talks we had with the Minister of Education and his aides in various departments, that they are well aware of the shortcomings and are working hard to correct them. In time, if all goes well, quality will match quantity.

If money can buy quality, then it will certainly be attained. For the Cuban government has indicated, by the fantastically large expenditures already invested in education, that it will meet the cost, no matter how great, of educating its people. Though exact education-budget figures are difficult to obtain because, in some instances, ministries other than Education, as well as mass organizations, make outlays for education, two facts are plain from the 1967 budget figure of $312,000,-000[12] given us by the Minister of Education:

1. Cuba is spending on education sums far in excess of what was spent before the Revolution—over four times as much.[13]

2. Cuba's per capita expenditure of $39 and per student expenditure of $141.21 is far in excess of that of all the Latin American countries as a whole: $39 compared to $6.13 per capita; and $141.21 compared to $35.62. It is also higher than that of Uruguay, whose per capita of $23.17 and per student expenditure of $126.31 is the highest in Latin America outside of Cuba.[14]

---

[12] This figure seems to correspond with those given in the Ministry of Education's 1967 Report to UNESCO, a pamphlet entitled *Cuba, 1967, The Educational Movement*, pp. 10-12, though the explanation in those pages is not too clear.

[13] The budget figure for 1956 was $74,200,000 (cf. Richard Jolly, in Dudley Seers (ed.), *Cuba, The Economic and Social Revolution*, p. 182).

[14] Cf. table in *Socio-Economic Progress in Latin America*, Sixth Annual Report (1966) Inter-American Development Bank, p. 39. The figures in this table may not be strictly comparable because the year is 1965 and private school expenditures may not be included; nevertheless, the picture shown in the comparison is valid enough.

Laurent Schwartz, Professor of Mathematics at the Faculty of Science in Paris, and one of the top mathematicians in the world today, was in Cuba while we were there. He had been in Brazil a little while before, and in an interview reported in *Granma*, March 3, 1968, he made an astonishing comparison between the two countries which made clear both the superiority of education in Cuba and its promise for the future:

"The universal and democratic character of education in this country is invaluable," the French mathematician added, stating that it is truly impressive how the educational level of the people is constantly being raised, thus assuring the groundwork for also raising the scientific level.

Schwartz cited a concrete example, the situation in Brazil. He compared Brazil's population of 80,000,000 with the 8,000,000 inhabitants of Cuba and pointed out that, despite the great differences in the populations of the two countries, the actual number of persons who obtain an education in Brazil is approximately the same as that of Cuba, since in Brazil the great majority of the people are illiterate and there are only primitive schools in the countryside. Therefore only certain sectors of the urban population get an education. He stated that the situation in Cuba was quite different, and, therefore, with a much smaller population Cuba can train more scientific cadres on a higher level than Brazil, a country he visited quite recently.

"The Revolution is giving tremendous stimulus to development. Within a short time—between 5 and 15 years—Cuba can have scientists of international caliber, precisely because this development has the backing of the Revolution."

The wretched of the earth need no longer live in darkness—illiteracy and ignorance *can* be eliminated. Given the opportunity to learn and to develop their talents, the masses can transform themselves and their society. Cuba's outstanding achievements in education are proof of the possibility of moving from underdevelopment to development once the imperialist yoke is removed.

# 3

# Health

As with education, so with health. In spite of the serious shortage of doctors, one-third of whom fled Cuba (and they are *still* leaving at the rate of four to six a month), in spite of the blockade which made medicine and equipment very difficult to obtain, nevertheless the progress made in the field of health highlights the fact that what must be done in the underdeveloped countries of Latin America can be achieved only by a genuine socialist revolution.

This is the case because socialist revolution makes possible sweeping changes which, particularly in the field of health, are so necessary to remedy the evils inherent in the capitalist system. Capitalist medicine is mainly concerned with curing sickness, and this is done magnificently for those who live where the doctors are in abundance and have money to pay; socialist medicine is mainly concerned with *preventing* illness for all the people, no matter where they live or how low their incomes.

In capitalist Cuba the one medical school stressed those

branches of medicine that would prove most profitable to graduate doctors. The subject of epidemiology was not even in the curriculum, and hygiene was treated superficially. In socialist Cuba the three medical schools do not concern themselves with what will be profitable to the graduate doctors but rather with what will benefit all the people—so epidemiology and hygiene are basic subjects.

In capitalist Cuba, as in all the Latin American countries today, the private practice of medicine with its emphasis on money-making was accompanied, in the public health sector, by inadequate and graft-ridden state and municipal institutions; in socialist Cuba, a plan for the entire country has been set up enabling the Ministry of Public Health to analyze needs, integrate previously scattered resources into one unit, and allocate priorities so as to promote the general health.

In capitalist Cuba, as in all other Latin American countries today, doctors and hospital beds were concentrated in the major urban centers, and it was not uncommon for thousands of unfortunate rural inhabitants to die because they could not afford to go where the medical help they needed was located; in socialist Cuba, the medical help needed by the inhabitants in the countryside is brought to them and is free. Since 1964 medical students have pledged (and it is now a requirement for the M.D. degree), that upon graduation they will not go into private practice, that their first two years as doctors will be spent in dispensaries and hospitals in remote rural areas.

"One of the most serious health problems," says the Inter-American Development Bank in its 1966 Report,[1] "is the shortage of medical personnel, aides and health centers in most Latin American countries, and the poor geographical distribution of available personnel and facilities."

Correct. The government of Cuba has tackled that "most

---

[1] *Op. cit.*, p. 24.

serious health problem" by changing that "poor geographical distribution of available personnel and facilities." In 1958, Cuba had one rural hospital with ten beds; today in socialist Cuba there are forty-seven rural hospitals with 1,300 beds, plus fifty medical and dental clinics, nonexistent before.

It will come as a surprise to many Americans to learn that the same "serious health problem" exists even in the United States and for the same reason—that not enough doctors are located where they are most needed, in the rural areas and in the ghettos. A letter to the *New York Times* on March 30, 1968, from Dr. Ira Marks of Chatham, New York, tells the story:

The infant mortality rate in this country is quite respectable when limited to our middle- and upper-class white urban community. However, it becomes absolutely disgraceful when one adds the rates from the black ghettos and rural America, particularly in the southeast.

This is not because these people cannot afford medical care, but rather because of the inadequate number and distribution of practicing physicians. (Medicaid really has not made any more doctors available in Harlem.) Offering Federal funds to pay for physicians' fees and to create new medical schools will not solve the problem of the unavailable physician unless the graduates of these new schools will actually practice medicine and be willing to serve in the ghetto and rural areas where they are needed.

If more money is to be spent for health services, let it be spent in the creation of new practitioner-oriented medical schools whose "clinics" would be physicians' offices in areas where none now exist, whose "professors" would include well-qualified practitioners of the art of medicine, and whose "research grants" would be spent gathering together and assisting into practice groups of physicians, both generalists and specialists, who would serve those areas most in need of health care.

After all we must not forget that any "℞ for Health Services"—

even a prepaid one—cannot help the ailing patient unless there is someone there to perform the service.

The kind of medical attention Dr. Marks is writing about may or may not come in the near future to the rich United States. It is already on its way in "underdeveloped"—but socialist—Cuba, where the number of hospitals has risen from 57 before the Revolution to 170 today, plus 250 polyclinics (health centers), previously unknown; beds available in hospitals and clinics have doubled, from 21,000 to 42,000, from 3.3 per 1,000 inhabitants to 5.4.[2] Of the nineteen other Latin American countries, only Argentina and Uruguay surpass the present Cuban figure for hospital beds.

What these bare statistics cannot reveal is the magnitude of the problem that was faced by the Ministry of Health at the advent of the Revolution. Of the 158 senior professors who had been teaching at the University of Havana Medical School, all but 17 fled the country. In the years immediately following the Revolution, over 2,000 practicing physicians, one-third of the total number, left. When the United States instituted its blockade, the flow of drugs, equipment, medical publications, nearly all of which had come from the United States, was abruptly cut off. But the health of the people, like their education, was considered of paramount importance, and with the government providing the needed funds, the medical fraternity providing the necessary effort, and the Ministry a rational public health plan, most of the difficulties were overcome.

Because of the population increase more of everything is needed—and it is being supplied. There are in Cuba today 7,000 doctors, 1,000 more than before the Revolution. Instead

[2] The statistics in this chapter on health in Cuba come from Ministry of Health documents and reports, or from interviews with officials in the Ministry.

of a student body of 3,500 with 350 graduates coming from the one medical school at Havana each year, today the three medical schools have a total student body of 5,000 from which 500 now graduate annually. It is interesting to note that 48 percent of all medical students are women.

The original teaching staff of 158 senior professors has been increased to 250 and, unlike before, both the teachers and the students devote themselves, full time, to the study of medicine alone. As Dr. Roberto Perada, Vice-Minister of Health, told us:

When I studied medicine before the Revolution, it was possible for a medical student to get his license without attending school, or even without any hospital practice. We had one microscope for eighty students; today there is one microscope for every six students, and there is constant contact with the hospitals, the laboratory, and the patients. Before 1959, I remember, there were frequently not enough beds in the hospitals, and patients often had to sleep on the floor. At times patients could not be admitted because there was no room even on the floor! Today, while we still don't have all the hospital facilities we need, no patients have to sleep on the floor.

Under the public health system in Cuba today, doctors do not make calls at the patient's home except in cases of emergency. Instead, the patient goes for examination and treatment to the polyclinic or rural dispensary nearest his home. If additional tests or consultations are required, the patient is referred to the regional hospital. If he needs to be hospitalized, he is sent to the regional hospital or, if necessary, to that major institute in Havana which specializes in his illness. The complete file on his case—all the records—are subsequently sent back to his original doctor and clinic which give him whatever follow-up care he may need.

In May, 1968, a friend of ours, Dr. David Spain, director of the department of pathology at the Brookdale Hospital Center, Brooklyn, was invited to lecture on his subject in Cuba. He wrote a report on his visit which touches on so many aspects of Cuban medical care that we are quoting it at length:

There are five general teaching hospitals in Havana, as well as several specialty teaching hospitals (obstetrics, pediatrics, and orthopedics). Many of these have been built since the Revolution, and most of the existing ones have been renovated and enlarged. These are modern, attractive, well-maintained structures. Each general teaching hospital contains a different specialty institute. This prevents wasteful duplication of resources and allows the best use of personnel.

I conducted seminars and made rounds in a number of institutes. One was the Cardiovascular Institute, in which the surgical program is directed by Dr. Noel González, a compassionate and able young surgeon. This program was started in 1964 with the aid of Dr. Bernardo Castro, a Mexican cardiovascular surgeon. Since then there have been 700 closed and 150 open heart operations. Over fifty pacemakers have been implanted. While on rounds I examined a patient who three months previously had two prosthetic valves inserted (tricuspid and mitral). I also saw the X-ray pictures of the valves in place. A Soviet modification of the Starr-Edwards valve was used. As far as I could determine these were functioning perfectly and the patient was walking around in seemingly good condition. In the Nephrology Institute (the General Surgical Hospital) Dr. Buch, the director, took me on extensive rounds, where I saw a wide variety of cases with acute and chronic renal failure. Dr. Buch was exceptionally well-informed in the most intricate and modern aspects of renal disease. About a hundred renal biopsies are performed annually on this service. They have not yet attempted renal transplants.

On rounds and during the seminars and lectures, the questions directed to me indicated a high level of understanding and ability in the practical aspects of medical diagnosis and care. I was repeatedly impressed by the rapport and the warmth of relationship that existed between physicians and patients. . . .

Because my chief host was Dr. Israel Borrajero, the chief pathologist, and because my specialty also is pathology, I was better able to evaluate the hospital laboratories and pathology departments. In 1958, in all of Cuba, there were twenty qualified pathologists. Following the Revolution only nine of them remained in the country. As a result of an intensive training program there are now sixty. Twelve more are required to meet the planned standards and current needs, but there are now thirty physicians in various stages of graduate training in pathology. All hospitals with major surgical programs are equipped to examine frozen sections. All major pathology departments have automatic tissue-processing equipment, mostly imported from England. In one of the general teaching hospitals in Havana there is a technician's school that provides competent personnel for the other hospitals. I examined the histological preparations at some of the hospitals and in most instances found them to be superior to sections prepared in many of the good laboratories in the United States. There are now fifty cytotechnicians and thirty more are in training. By 1970, the cytology screening program for cervical cancer will test 400,000 women annually. Carcinoma *in situ* is detected in one percent of those examined. In a nation with close to eight million people, where 40 percent are under the age of fifteen, this is a considerable achievement. Eighty-five percent of all deaths are autopsied, and microscopic examinations are made of all surgically removed tissue. There is ample blood available for the blood banks because one pint is obtained from the family of every patient admitted to a hospital. Each hospital has a tissue committee.

The chief pathologist, Dr. Borrajero, a dedicated and competent doctor, receives a monthly salary of 750 pesos (U. S. equivalent: $750). His salary is at the top of the scale but its purchasing power must be evaluated against the fact that rent is fixed at 10 percent of one's salary regardless of its level and regardless of the type of home. It is expected that within a few years all housing will be rent-free. Many other services such as telephone, medical care, and education are already entirely free.

Most of the physicians I met seemed to be satisfied to work

within this framework. There are ample opportunities for further training and promotion. All physicians receive a one-month vacation a year and time off for continuing education. The lower end of the salary scale is about 300 pesos a month, which is the salary of a research trainee. There still remains a small group of discontented physicians and some of these are leaving the country.

The picture in obstetric care represents perhaps one of the great successes of the entire medical program. Currently over 80 percent of all deliveries—95 percent in Havana—are performed in hospitals by physicians. In the uncomplicated cases, natural childbirth with the use of local anesthesia and minimal sedation is the accepted method. A new program designed to save medical manpower and to insure a more efficient distribution of adequate obstetric care consists of training obstetric nurses to manage cases that reveal no prenatal complications and in which no problems are anticipated during labor. There has been a sharp decline in both the neonatal and maternal mortality rates. Dr. Valdez-Vivo, Professor of Obstetrics and Gynecology, who had spent ten years in this specialty in Chicago before his return to Cuba, told me that the latest national figures, as yet unpublished, revealed a neonatal mortality rate slightly higher than 2 percent and a maternal mortality rate under 0.7 per 1,000. These are probably the lowest rates in all of Latin America. Some maternity homes have been built near the rural obstetrics hospitals so that women in the last month of pregnancy may live adjacent to the hospital to avoid transportation difficulties. Provision is also made for a short stay at these homes after discharge from the hospital. . . .

The annual number of medical examinations prior to 1958 is not known, but the marked increase in medical utilization and availability is noted by an increase from twelve million examinations in 1963 to nineteen million in 1967. Dental care, which had been available only to the wealthier population, has expanded considerably in the past eight years. Although much still remains to be done in this area, there are currently forty dental clinics where none existed previously, and a new dental school—

in addition to the one in Havana—has been developed in Santa Clara.

The most vivid experience of my stay in Cuba was a visit to the Psychiatric Institute on the outskirts of Havana. Prior to 1958 this was an old-fashioned snake-pit situation in which 5,000 chronic mental patients received minimal custodial care. It has been rebuilt into an open, spacious, modern, and attractive facility with a baseball field equipped for night playing, an outdoor movie theater, many classrooms, art shops, workshops, cultural areas, farms, and flower gardens. About twenty percent of the patients remain hospitalized for severe illness. In the other areas of the hospital, every patient was active and busy, with no one in bed or in the wards; I felt that I was visiting an adult work or cultural camp. There are no fences or guards in sight. The patients operate one of the largest scientific chicken farms in Cuba. I spent an hour in the auditorium where patients are involved all day with music, dance, singing, etc. Before we left, over fifty patients volunteered to perform for us. It appears that, within the limits of their chronic psychiatric illness, these patients are living constructive lives in an orderly and integrated community.[3]

We also visited this famous mental hospital and were just as impressed as Dr. Spain. Any American who has read the reports of the pitiful conditions, the horrors perpetrated in the mental institutions of the United States, with all its wealth, would have to be impressed—and ashamed—on seeing what is undoubtedly one of the best hospitals of its kind in the world in the poor, "underdeveloped" country of Cuba.

How important public health is to socialist Cuba can be gauged by the budget allocated to health—from 21 million pesos before the Revolution to 158 million in 1967, almost eight times as much in only eight years.

A planned system of public health with the major emphasis

---

[3] For the full report, see *Medical Tribune*, Vol. 9, Nos. 60 and 61 (July 25 and July 29, 1968).

on prevention instead of cure, free medical care, doctors and nurses and dentists and hospitals where they are needed—even if costs skyrocket—this is the health program in socialist Cuba. And it works. The statistics prove that a revolutionary approach to the problem can bring down sickness and death rates in the short space of eight years in a way that is not possible in a Latin America without socialism.

Gastroenteritis has long been prevalent in Cuba and in other Latin American countries. It has been one of the five leading causes of death, and still is. The rate per 100,000 inhabitants in Colombia is 105.4, in Guatemala 229, in Venezuela 64.4, and in Peru 103.5. In Cuba it had been brought down to 50.8 in 1962, four years after the Revolution; in another four years, in 1966, the figure had been reduced to 19.6. That reduction from 50.8 to 19.6, in just four years, *saved over 2,500 lives.*

Due to the great work done by Drs. Salk and Sabin, it is now possible to get rid of the dread disease of polio, yet no Latin American country has succeeded in eliminating it—except Cuba. There has been not one single case of polio in Cuba for the past three years.

Malaria is still a big killer in Central America, Brazil, Colombia, Venezuela, as it was in Cuba before the Revolution when there were 7,000-10,000 cases annually. There were 3,519 cases in Cuba in 1962; there were only 10 in 1967.

High among the causes of death in Latin America is typhoid fever. There were 1,158 cases in Cuba in 1964; in 1966 there were only 167.

Cuba's phenomenal successes in cutting sickness and death rates are made possible because the Ministry of Public Health can do what cannot be done in the capitalist countries of Latin America—mobilize the entire country in a nationwide campaign to do what needs to be done. Not only the trade unions, but the Cuban Women's Federation, the neighborhood Committees for the Defense of the Revolution, and all the other mass organizations are enrolled in the tremendous task of mass vaccination for children. In 1964, they helped to administer anti-polio vaccine to 2,450,000 children under fourteen years of age; in 1966, to 1,407,000 children under six. Every year, hundreds of thousands of children are vaccinated against smallpox, tuberculosis, diphtheria, whooping cough, tetanus, and typhoid.

With what results? Perhaps the best illustration of the success of the health program in socialist Cuba is the infant mortality rate which, the Report of the Inter-American Development Bank informs us,[4] "in nine Latin American countries exceeds 80 per thousand live births, and in two countries is in excess of 100 per thousand live births." In no other Latin American country is infant mortality less than 42 per thousand live births. But in Cuba, in 1966, it was 37.7 (for non-whites in the United States, in 1966, it was 36.7; for whites, 20.6).

Mass organizations play a big role in another program which is helping to improve the health of the Cuban people: the program of physical education, sports, and recreation. The philosophy behind this program, which is under the jurisdiction of INDER (the National Institute of Sports, Physical Education, and Recreation), is that "the evidence of science and the accumulated experience of today's world clearly show that systematic practice of physical activities produces organic, functional, psychological, moral, and social changes of a fundamental nature. These coincide with and contribute to a balanced development. . . ."[5]

If it's good for the health of our people, then they must have

---

[4] *Op. cit.*, p. 23.
[5] *Cuba: Man, Revolution, op. cit.*, p. 29.

it, is the approach; not only school children or professional teams, but workers, farmers, young people, old people, men, women. So today some two million Cubans, one-quarter of the entire population, participate regularly in some form of sports activity—not watching other people play, but playing themselves.

It is true that in spite of the tremendous increase in medical personnel, in hospitals, and in equipment, everything is still in short supply. The old-timers have gone, the new doctors and nurses and technicians need experience. The scientific tradition is still in its infancy. But though much still remains to be done, the accomplishments of Cuba in the field of health are already many and great. Of utmost importance is the new approach: people are treated like human beings entitled to the best care, whether they are rich or poor. The guiding principle was expressed by Che: "One human life is worth more than all the wealth of the richest man in the world."

In health, Cuba is a lesson to the underdeveloped countries —that without a socialist revolution there is no possibility of going beyond the introduction of largely ineffectual reforms which may ease the pain somewhat but won't cure the disease.

# 4

# The Urge to Diversify

When we interviewed President Dorticós in the Presidential Palace on the morning of March 9, we began by telling him how enormously impressed we were by Cuba's achievements in the fields of education and health in the years since we wrote *Cuba: Anatomy of a Revolution;* and we asked him to tell us about the country's great achievements in the economic field. He said that it would be vanity on his part to claim that there were any. He was being too modest. There have been some remarkable achievements in the economic field and in all probability there will be even more remarkable ones in the future. But before we go into that, let us review briefly the stages through which the Revolution has passed since the conquest of power on January 1, 1959. In this chapter we discuss the period 1959-1963, and in the following chapter the period from 1963 to the present.

The story of Cuba's grotesque underdevelopment and ruthless exploitation by United States imperialism—opposite sides of the same coin—has been told many times and will not be repeated here.[1] Suffice it to recall that sugar accounted for about a quarter of Cuba's gross national product and four-fifths of its exports, and that trade with the United States accounted for by far the largest part of both exports and imports. Few countries have been as dependent on one crop and one trading partner as was pre-revolutionary Cuba. And in few has the resultant contradiction between grossly under-utilized land and manpower on the one hand and abject poverty on the other been more glaring.

In these circumstances it is not surprising that the Cuban independence movement, going back to the time of José Martí in the late nineteenth century, was passionately devoted not only to political sovereignty but also to economic diversification, interpreting this term in just about every possible sense. Cuba should raise many crops, including enough of everything it needed to feed its people; it should have real industries of its own (as distinct from finishing operations attached to foreign producers of materials and components) which would supply the home market and give employment to Cuban workers; it should trade freely with the whole world and not merely with one monopolistic overlord.

These ideas were inherited and further developed by Fidel Castro and his comrades in the July 26th Movement, and when they came to power they quite naturally acted upon them. The guiding principles of economic policy in the first years of the Revolution were thus agricultural diversification, industrialization, and the cultivation of new trading partners.

---

[1] A brief summary will be found in our book *Cuba: Anatomy of a Revolution* (New York and London: Monthly Review Press, 1960), Chapters 2 and 3. A more recent account is in Edward Boorstein's *The Economic Transformation of Cuba: A First-Hand Account* (New York and London: Monthly Review Press, 1968), especially Chapter 1.

It is often said nowadays that these early efforts at diversification were a failure, and in an important sense this is certainly true. This should not, however, cause us to lose sight of the very important accomplishments of the period. Mass purchasing power was greatly increased in the first half of 1959 by rent and price reductions in the cities, by the first Agrarian Reform in the countryside (which completely abolished agricultural rents), and by the initiation of numerous construction projects (housing, roads, tourist centers, etc.) all over the island. The result, of course, was a steep increase in demand for all sorts of consumer goods, and both agriculture and industry responded to this stimulus with considerable success. Table 5 shows the growth in production of a number of agricultural commodities which figure prominently in mass consumption.

Table 5

Production of Certain Agricultural Commodities
(thousands of metric tons)

|  | *1958* | *1961* | *1962* | *percent increase 1958-1962* |
|---|---|---|---|---|
| Beans | 33 | 59 | 78 | 136 |
| Rice | 163 | 213 | 320 | 96 |
| Corn | 134 | 198 | 257 | 92 |
| Tobacco | 42 | 52 | 59 | 40 |
| Potatoes | 63 | 97 | 92 | 46 |
| Beef | 169 | 207 | n.a.[a] | 23  (1958-61) |

[a] not available.

*Source:* Michel Gutelman, *L'agriculture socialisée à Cuba* (Paris: François Maspero, 1967), p. 158.

It is worth noting that through 1961 these impressive gains were made simultaneously with an increase in sugar production—in 1961 the sugar harvest yielded 6.9 million metric tons, the second largest amount in Cuban history, and it was only in 1962 that sugar production went down. There were several reasons for this, among which perhaps the most important was the plowing up of sugar lands to grow other crops.

In these same years industrial production also increased, but most of the increase resulted from greater utilization of already existing capacity rather than from the establishment of new industries. As of August, 1962, according to a speech by Fidel Castro to a National Production Conference, only ten new factories had been built by the Revolution: a non-ferrous smelting plant, several textile mills, some tomato canning plants, a pencil factory, and a plant for making stuffed dolls.[2] Some twenty additional factories were then under construction, including a relatively large establishment for producing household utensils and appliances, a steel foundry, plants for producing picks and shovels, barbed wire, locks, knives and forks, brushes, kenaf bags, plastics, animal feed, antibiotics, salt, cocoa, and more canned tomatoes.[3] For the most part, the choice of factories to be built was dictated by a combination of need for the products and a hoped-for substitution of domestic products for imports.

It was in the third aspect of diversification—the development of new trading partners—that Cuba had the greatest successes in the early years of the Revolution. Following a modest opening of trade relations with the Soviet Union in 1959 and early 1960, the whole situation was drastically changed by the bitter economic warfare which broke out be-

---

[2] Boorstein, *op. cit.*, p. 119.
[3] *Ibid.*, pp. 119-120.

tween Cuba and the United States in the summer of 1960.
Cuba had arranged to buy oil from the USSR, but the U.S.-
owned refineries refused to process it. Cuba retaliated by
taking over the refineries, and the United States then can-
celled the Cuban sugar quota, leaving Cuba with some three
million tons of unsold sugar. It was at this juncture that the
Soviet Union and the other socialist countries stepped in in
a big way, providing a market for Cuban sugar and in general taking the place of the United States as Cuba's leading
customers and suppliers. No less important, the socialist
countries became a vital source of credits at a time when
Cuba's ability to export lagged far behind her need for imports. A good idea of how important economic relations
between Cuba and the socialist countries had become by the
summer of 1962 is provided by Table 6.

Trade data for later years confirm the impression con-
veyed by this table that in acquiring new trading partners
Cuba was not becoming completely dependent on any one
country as it had been in the pre-revolutionary period. Imports from the USSR have normally been about half of
Cuba's total imports, and exports to the USSR a somewhat
smaller proportion. The rest of Cuba's foreign trade has
tended to be roughly divided between the other socialist
countries and a considerable number of capitalist countries
(among which Spain, Japan, France, Britain, and Canada
have played the most important roles). In this respect, then,
Cuba has made important progress in satisfying her deep-
seated urge to diversify.

Despite this achievement—and the more modest gains in
agricultural diversification and industrialization discussed
above—it must be admitted that the economic policy of the
first years of the Revolution was a failure in the crucially
important sense that it did not provide or point the way to
a viable strategy of economic development. The initial hope

Table 6

Credits to Cuba from the Socialist Countries

| Countries | Credits (million $) | Annual interest (percent) | Use | Years for amortization |
|---|---|---|---|---|
| USSR | 100 | 2.5 | Technical and scientific assistance in the nickel and cobalt industries, with equipment, instruments, machinery | 5 |
| USSR | 100 | 2.5 | Petroleum refineries, iron and steel plants, electrical installations, geological surveys, services | 12 |
| China | 60 | 0.0 | Industrial plants and equipment, machinery and tools | 10 |
| Czechoslovakia | 40 | 2.5 | Machinery and industrial equipment, electric plants, automotive industries | 10 |
| Hungary | 15 | 2.5 | Industrial plants, machinery and equipment, tools | 10 |
| Rumania | 15 | 2.5 | Machinery, industrial plants and equipment, electric installations | from 1966 on |
| Poland | 12 | 2.5 | Industrial plants and equipment, shipyard | 8 |
| East Germany | 10 | 2.5 | Industrial plants, shops, and varied equipment | 10 |
| Bulgaria | 5 | 2.5 | Industrial plants, refrigerating plants, hydraulic installations | 10 |
| **Total** | 357 | | | |

Source: Bohemia, August 17, 1962. Reproduced in Dudley Seers (ed.), Cuba: The Economic and Social Revolution (Chapel Hill: University of North Carolina Press, 1964), p. 313.

had been that through diversification and industrialization Cuba would be able to reduce drastically her need for imports. The need for exports would also be reduced, but not to the same degree in the near future, since Cuba would have to pay off the credits extended, mainly by the socialist countries, in the period of industrialization. Later on, however, with the credits repaid, with a strong industrial base and a diversified agriculture, Cuba would be able to enter upon a long period of vigorous and balanced growth relying primarily, if not entirely, on her own resources. Sugar, long the hated symbol of imperialist domination, would be relegated to a secondary role; and modern industry would take its rightful place as the motor force of true economic development. It was not uncommon in those days to encounter projections of overall annual growth rates of 15 percent, a favorable balance of trade by 1965, and an equilibrium in the balance of payments before the end of the decade. After that everything would be plain sailing.

These optimistic hopes were understandable at the time.[4] Pre-revolutionary Cuba was characterized by a scandalous underutilization of resources: probably less than half of the arable land was effectively cultivated; unemployment averaged at least 25 percent of the labor force; and many enterprises had ample inventories of materials and finished products. Under these circumstances production was able, as we have seen, to spurt forward under the powerful stimulus of the expanded mass purchasing power which the Revolution let loose. Edward Boorstein, who held key posts in the revolutionary government's economic agencies during the period 1960–1963, gives an apt summary of the situation:

---

[4] We shared them. See *Cuba: Anatomy of a Revolution*, especially Chapter 13 and Epilogue.

The rapid progress of the Cuban economy in the early years after the Revolution took power was made possible by the reserves. The very irrationality of the prerevolutionary economy served as a springboard for advance. By using the excess capacity of the construction industry and idle labor, you could produce schools, hospitals, and houses. By giving unemployed labor access to idle or under-utilized land, you could get quick increases in agricultural output. Because of the excess capacity, you could make industrial output go up more than 15 percent in the first year of the Revolution. You could cut out luxury foreign-exchange expenditures by a small part of the population and save tens of millions of dollars.[5]

It is not surprising that these early successes engendered an atmosphere of optimism in which anything seemed possible. But unfortunately this soon proved to be an illusion. As production in one line after another bumped up against the ceilings imposed by existing resources, all sorts of bottlenecks began to develop with which the Cuban economy, lacking an effective planning apparatus and seriously weakened by the United States blockade and the departure of many technicians and other trained personnel, was quite unable to cope. In these circumstances the advances of the early years were checked and in many cases turned into declines. The sugar harvest, for example, after reaching the near-record level of 6.9 million metric tons in 1961, fell sharply to 4.8 million in 1962 and 3.8 million in 1963—a decline of 45 percent in two years. This decline in sugar production was one, but only one, factor in causing a drastic worsening of Cuba's balance of payments. Table 7 shows what happened.

Note that the deficit was a compound of a decline in exports and an increase in imports: exports dropped 16 percent in two years, while imports rose 19 percent. "The balance-

---

[5] Boorstein, *op. cit.*, p. 82.

Table 7
Exports and Imports
(millions of dollars)

|  | Exports | Imports | Surplus (+) or deficit (—) |
|---|---|---|---|
| 1960 | 618.2 | 579.9 | + 38.3 |
| 1961 | 624.9 | 638.7 | — 13.8 |
| 1962 | 520.6 | 690.2 | —169.6 |

Source: Edward Boorstein, The Economic Transformation of Cuba (New York and London: Monthly Review Press, 1968), p. 130.

of-payments deficit," in Boorstein's words, "became Cuba's central economic problem; it reflected and accentuated the key difficulties of the whole economy."[6]

By this time (1962) it was already clear that import substitution through industrialization, from which so much had initially been expected, would provide no solution to the balance-of-payments problem and in fact might even contribute to making it worse for a long time to come. The reason was not only that starting the industries in question required large imports of machinery and equipment but also that in most cases operation of the newly established industries depended on imported raw materials, fuel, replacement parts, etc. The net result was little or no gain in substituting national production for imports.

There were other reasons, too, why the early enthusiasm for industrialization cooled off with experience. Technicians, administrators, skilled workers—all kinds of qualified manpower—were scarce or nonexistent. Much of the plant and

---

[6] Ibid., pp. 132-133. Boorstein's discussion of this whole problem—especially in his chapter entitled "Mounting Pressure Against Resources" (Chapter 4)—is highly recommended.

equipment acquired from the socialist countries turned out to be of poor quality. But above all it became increasingly obvious that Cuba's demand for industrial products was not, and under no conceivable circumstances could become, large enough to justify the establishment of a wide variety of modern, technologically efficient industries. By committing herself to a program of industrial diversification, Cuba would in effect be condemning herself to industrial backwardness.

Clearly, the situation called for a new strategy of economic development. The country's historical urge to diversify had been vigorously acted upon and had produced many valuable results and even more valuable experience. But with the balance of payments in long-term deficit—an implicit threat to Cuba's newly won independence—and with the sanguine hopes of the early period frustrated, the Revolution faced a crisis which only new ideas and courageous action could hope to overcome.

# 5

# The New Strategy of Development

In looking for a way out of the economic crisis in which they found themselves in 1962, the Cuban leaders were forced to re-examine all the assumptions on which they had been operatting. And the central conclusion they came to was that if, under then existing conditions, a combination of agricultural diversification and industrialization wouldn't work, they would have to fall back on agricultural specializaton. Having reached this conclusion, they asked themselves how it could be implemented without condemning the country to a future of dependency and underdevelopment similar to its past. And this in turn led to the formulation of an entirely new strategy of development.

Sugar and cattle were selected as the main areas of agricultural specialization, in both cases because natural conditions of soil and climate are particularly favorable and in the case of sugar because of accumulated know-how and the existence of a large processing industry. More sugar would be sold abroad to solve the balance-of-payments problem. For some years expanded production of meat and dairy products would be mostly consumed domestically, but eventually meat would also become a major export item. For the near future investment policy would be dictated by the needs of these two sectors: this would hold not only for agricultural investments as such, but also for investments in industry and infrastructure. In the latter spheres, the guiding purpose would be to meet the needs of an expanding agriculture for such things as fertilizers, electric power, processing facilities, workers' houses, silos and barns, roads, water for irrigation, and so on. All this was regarded not as a permanent substitute for general agricultural and industrial diversification but as a necessary preliminary. Sugar and cattle would be rationalized and mechanized as rapidly as possible with a view to vastly increased yields per man and per acre. In this way, after a transition period land and labor would be released for other uses and the direction of investment could be shifted to other crops and other industries.

The feasibility of this development strategy depended, of course, on the existence of a reliable *and expanding* market for Cuba's sugar. Before the Revolution, the United States quota system gave Cuba a reliable market but not an expanding one, so that the strategy conceived in 1962 would have been out of the question in those days. But now things were obviously very different. Cuba was already part of the international socialist system, and it had been proved that the socialist countries could, if they wanted to, provide a market for Cuban sugar. Everyone recognized, however, that their buying a large part of the Cuban output beginning in the middle of 1960 was in the nature of a life-saving operation, undertaken for political reasons. There were no guarantees that this situation would continue or that the prices the socialist countries would be willing to pay for Cuban sugar would hold up in the future. So the Cubans set out to discover whether the socialist market for Cuban sugar could be turned into the guaranteed, expanding, remunerative outlet they needed.

Perhaps some day the story will be told of the discussions and negotiations which took place between Havana and Moscow in 1962 and 1963. It should make fascinating reading. To what extent did the ideas embodied in the agreement which was finally signed on January 21, 1964, originate with the Cubans and to what extent with the Russians? We know the urgent economic problems which motivated the Cubans, but we know next to nothing about the thinking of the Russians. Were their motives primarily political, as most people seem to have assumed, or did economic considerations play as important a part with them as with the Cubans?

Whatever the answers to these questions, it is important to understand that Soviet economic policies toward Cuba, centering on the sugar agreement of 1964, are in no sense charity but on the contrary may well yield substantial long-run economic benefits to the USSR. There are several factors which combine to produce this conclusion: (1) Because of the nature of its soil and climate the Soviet Union is not and probably never will be a low-cost agricultural producer, and it is certain that it is a high-cost producer of sugar. (2) Again because of soil and climate, but also because of historical specialization, Cuba is a low-cost producer of sugar, perhaps the lowest-cost producer in the world.[1] (3) The Soviet Union

---

[1] So far as we know, no detailed study of comparative costs of sugar production in Cuba and the USSR has been carried out. Michel Gutelman believes that "costs of production are much higher in the Soviet Union. According to René Dumont [a well-known French agronomist], in the Ukraine, with yields of twenty tons of sugar beet per hectare, the costs would be double those of Cuba. 'Some people,' he adds, 'estimate that the average costs of production in the Soviet Union

*is* a low-cost producer of the things Cuba is most in need of: oil, trucks and jeeps, tractors, machinery, etc. (4) It follows that if prices are set in reasonable relation to costs, the Soviet Union can reduce the average cost of its sugar consumption by exchanging what Cuba needs for Cuban sugar—the more so the larger the quantities involved. (5) Furthermore, since the Soviet Union is in a phase of economic development characterized by rapid growth of sugar consumption,[2] this result can be attained without endangering existing Soviet investments in the growing and processing of sugar beets: all that need be done is to slow down the rate of growth of domestic sugar production.

So in addition to political reasons, the argument of economic advantage may well have played a part in the Soviet Union's decision to enter into the sugar agreement with Cuba. According to its terms, the Soviet Union committed itself to taking the following quantities of Cuban sugar (in millions of metric tons):

| | |
|------|-----|
| 1965 | 2.1 |
| 1966 | 3.0 |
| 1967 | 4.0 |
| 1968 | 5.0 |
| 1969 | 5.0 |
| 1970 | 5.0 |

are higher than 16 cents a pound.' On this assumption, the costs in the USSR would be more than three times as great as in Cuba and would exceed by far both prices on the world market and prices paid to Cuba." (*L'Agriculture socialisée à Cuba*, p. 215.)

[2] Even with the large amounts of sugar imported from Cuba, Soviet production grew from 5.8 million metric tons in 1960 to 9.6 million in 1965, an average annual increase of more than 13 percent (*Statistical Abstract of the United States*, 1967, p. 877). Since Cuban sugar data are normally expressed in metric tons, we have changed the *Statistical Abstract*'s short tons into metric tons (about 10 percent heavier) to facilitate comparisons.

The price was fixed for the duration of the agreement at 6.11 cents a pound. This was somewhat higher than the prices Cuban producers had been receiving for quota sugar in the United States market prior to the break between the two countries, and it compares with the following world market prices, as calculated by the Cubans and presented by Prime Minister Castro in his speech at the University of Havana on March 13, 1968 (in cents per pound):

| | |
|---|---|
| 1963 | 8.48 |
| 1964 | 5.86 |
| 1965 | 2.12 |
| 1966 | 1.86 |
| 1967 | 1.99 |
| 1963-67 (*avg.*) | 3.39 |

The other socialist countries soon concluded similar sugar agreements with Cuba. China agreed to take amounts reaching one million tons by 1970 at the same price of 6.11 cents a pound; and somewhat smaller quantities at slightly lower prices would go to the socialist countries of Eastern Europe.

With the strategy of development decided and the question of markets for sugar answered, Cuba's number one problem became the expansion of sugar production. And, in fact, before the agreements with the socialist countries were signed, Fidel had dramatized the issue by announcing a goal of ten million tons by 1970.

When you stop to think that the most sugar Cuba had ever produced was 7.2 million tons (in 1952), that since 1960 much sugar land had been switched to other crops, that the machinery and equipment in the mills had been allowed to deteriorate, that many technicians had left the country, that production was down to 3.8 million tons in 1963—when you stop to think of all this, you can understand the ambitious nature of the goal of ten million tons by 1970.[3] But this was not the only demanding task the revolutionary leadership set for the country. Cattle-raising, as already noted, was assigned a role second only to that of sugar in the new development strategy. In the words of Michel Gutelman:

In 1964 the broad outlines of an ambitious perspective plan for cattle were sketched out. The number of head of cattle would be raised from 6.6 million to 12 million in 1975. The latter would have a structure which would permit the annual slaughter of 4 million head and the daily production of 30 million liters of milk. To achieve this there was envisaged a considerable improvement in the alimentary base through transformation of natural into artificial pastures, the raising of the genetic quality of the herds by means of artificial insemination, and, finally, considerable investment in industrial installations.[4]

As for other agricultural products, the new development strategy called for cutting back on most of the "new" crops—that is, those which had been introduced or greatly expanded in the diversification drive of the first years (rice, corn, cotton, peanuts, etc.). These would again be supplied mainly through imports, the calculation being that the land, labor, and other resources devoted to their production would yield much more value if diverted to the production of sugar. But efforts would continue to be made to increase the production of those food-stuffs which figure prominently in the people's diet and/or which could not be conveniently imported (e.g., root vegetables, eggs, and poultry). Finally, exportable crops other than sugar—notably tobacco, coffee, and citrus fruits—with which Cuba had had past experience would also be expanded. With

---

[3] There is a good discussion of the technical revolution in the sugar industry implied by the ten-million-ton goal in Edward Boorstein's, *The Economic Transformation of Cuba,* pp. 206-209.

[4] Michel Gutelman, *op cit.,* p. 179.

respect to coffee and citrus fruits, targets have been raised sharply in the last couple of years; and, following a quarrel with the Chinese over rice imports in the winter of 1965-1966, the policy of cutting back rice production was reversed, though the aim still falls short of full self-sufficiency. The following is the latest official statement of crop targets for 1970, taken from a report submitted by the Cuban Delegation to the Rome Conference of the Food and Agriculture Organization (FAO) in late 1967:[5]

(a) To produce ten million metric tons of sugar.

(b) To satisfy all domestic needs for root vegetables, other vegetables, and fruit. To obtain exportable surpluses of the last two groups of products.

(c) To produce 90,000 metric tons of coffee.

(d) To have 65,000 hectares of beans and 200,000 hectares of rice under cultivation on state lands.

(e) To meet all the needs of the textile industry with domestic raw materials.

(f) To plant 100,000 hectares in citrus fruits that meet world productivity [quality?] levels.

(g) To plant more thousands of hectares of tobacco.

At about the same time that the new strategy of economic development was being worked out, the Cuban leaders launched a program of far-reaching organizational reform. For many reasons—to mention only the most important: a shortage of trained personnel, the danger of sabotage by counter-revolutionaries, the need for economic decisions and actions to conform to the political line of the Revolution—a high degree of centralization had been an inescapable characteristic of the early stages of the Revolution. It is hardly an exaggeration to say that, with the exception of financial affairs, the entire

---

[5] *Agricultural and Livestock Production in Cuba, 1965-1967*, (mimeographed, in English), p. 21.

economy was put under the control of one agency, the Institute of Agrarian Reform (INRA), itself manned largely by members of the Rebel Army. Within INRA there developed, at first spontaneously and then in a more formalized manner, what Michel Gutelman has called a "sectoralized" structure.[6] For example, one department was responsible for Cane Farms and another for People's Farms, which produced other crops (later these two forms were unified as State Farms). Industry came under the jurisdiction of the Department of Industrialization (later the Ministry of Industry), which in turn was divided into branches and trusts. All these sectors built up their own apparatuses reaching from the top down to the provinces and regions, and each was more or less jealous of its independence and prerogatives. Coordination was difficult— and often impossible—to achieve, and what there was of it tended to take place not at the operating level but at the higher bureaucratic levels. Thus, for example, on a Cane Farm at the end of the harvest there might be surpluses of men and equipment, while at the same time there might be shortages at a nearby People's Farm producing different crops. The existing organizational structure provided no way to solve this simple problem: what might happen in practice was either that nothing would be done or that the department of INRA responsible for People's Farms would scrounge around and find some or all of the needed men and equipment on other People's Farms, perhaps located many miles away in other districts or provinces. In either case, there would be an obvious and totally unnecessary waste of resources.

The situation was no better in industry, and changing INRA's Department of Industrialization into the Ministry of

---

[6] Gutelman's book contains by far the best description and analysis we have seen of these organizational problems and changes. See especially Parts 3 and 4, pp. 69-148.

Industry early in 1961 hardly helped matters. Having all industry under the centralized control of one agency in Havana could not but be an unwieldy and inefficient arrangement. And taken together with the sectoral organization of agriculture, it made effective coordination of the two spheres virtually impossible.

The reform of the agricultural structure was accomplished from approximately mid-1963 to mid-1964. Its aim was not decentralization, though a certain amount of that was necessarily involved, but rather de-sectoralization. All farms owned by the state were now reclassified as State Farms and grouped together on a geographical basis into *agrupaciones*. At the time of the Second Agrarian Reform (October, 1963) the boundaries of the State Farms were rationalized and the newly nationalized land was incorporated into them. The *agrupación* now became a key administrative and managerial unit, controlling the State Farms under it and responsible to a provincial administrator. The six provincial administrations were in turn responsible to the national office in Havana. In 1966 there were 58 *agrupaciones* containing 575 State Farms which ranged in size from 13,000 to 100,000 hectares (1 hectare = 2.47 acres). And by this time INRA was in all but name a regular ministry.[7]

This reform permitted the liquidation of the old system of sectoralization and the dispersal of most of the personnel in the top office to the province, *agrupación*, or State Farm

---

[7] We spent much time at INRA when we were in Cuba in 1960 and got to know it as a huge, bustling organization occupying the whole of one of the largest buildings on the Plaza de la Revolución, to and from which delegations and individuals from all over the island were constantly coming and going. When we went back to INRA in 1968, we found it relocated in much smaller quarters in the old city, to all appearances a quite ordinary and not particularly busy or important government office.

levels. It also eliminated many of the irrationalities of sector-alization. Take, for example, the case of the Cane Farm and the People's Farm given above: both would now be State Farms under the jurisdiction of a single *agrupación* whose function, among others, is to see that men and equipment are assigned where they are most needed within its territory.

With respect both to industry and to the relationship between industry and agriculture, the guiding principle of the new set-up was "integration." Here it will be useful to quote at some length from Gutelman's very interesting discussion of this principle. What he says is of great help in understanding the organizational philosophy of the Cuban Revolution. The new principle of organization involves

recognition of the necessity of linking the whole process of production to its material base, suppressing artificial obstacles stemming from administrative methods. In this spirit, the clear-cut separation between the spheres of agriculture, industry, transportation, internal commerce, and external commerce was condemned. The logical consequence of this condemnation would be a more or less complete liquidation of the Ministries of Foreign Commerce and Industry. . . .

To replace these ministries, and to correspond to the different types of production, it was proposed to organize flexible entities with functions and responsibilities in the fields of production, processing, transport, domestic distribution, and import and export. These entities would constitute veritable combines, vertically integrated from production to distribution. To the extent possible, these combines would have a national character—that is to say, they would depend directly on the Central Planning Commission without any intermediaries. Where it was impossible to distinguish clearly a line running from production up, these combines would be attached to a central organism like a ministry. The combine system seemed to be valid for a large number of productive activities whether or not linked to agriculture.[8]

---

[8] Gutelman, *op. cit.*, pp. 129-130.

In carrying out these ideas, some combines or combine-like entities were set up independently: this was notably the case with eggs and tobacco. Some were organized within INRA. And some were grouped under five new ministries which took the place of the Ministry of Industry: the Ministries of Mining and Metallurgy, Basic Industry, Light Industry, Food, and Sugar. Of course, there were many compromises and deviations from the underlying principle, and there have naturally been various changes in later years. Still, it seems that "integration" was a genuine operating principle and that it remains so and is likely to continue to remain so for the foreseeable future.

By the end of 1965, then, the Cuban Revolution had found its way both in terms of development strategy and organizational structure. It has traveled some distance since without deviating in essentials from the route mapped out in the transitional years 1963, 1964, and 1965.

# 6

# Economic Achievements, 1959-1968

One of the economic achievements of the Cuban Revolution
has been a great improvement in the comprehensiveness and
accuracy of statistics on production, consumption, trade, etc.
The Central Planning Commission (Junta Central de Planificación: JUCEPLAN) gathers these statistics and makes them
available to all interested government and Party agencies.
However, these compendia are not public documents and are
therefore not available for citation. The reasons for this are
the United States blockade and a natural desire on the part of
the Cubans not to make it easier for the various intelligence
agencies in Washington to keep tabs on what is happening on
the island. Nevertheless, the Cubans do make a good deal of
statistical and other economic information public—in speeches
of Fidel and other leaders, in reports to the United Nations
and its specialized agencies, and in articles in newspapers and
periodicals. In addition, officials are often glad to furnish
information on request, specifying what can and what cannot
be published. In our case we were particularly fortunate to

have a long interview with President Dorticós who, as head of JUCEPLAN, probably has a clearer view of the total economic picture than anyone else, with the possible exception of Fidel himself. And finally, since most countries publish detailed foreign trade data, much useful information about Cuba can be gathered from non-Cuban sources. In what follows, we have tried to select a few facts and figures from these various sources which will allow the reader to discern the broad contours of Cuban economic development during these years.

SUGAR

Cuban sugar production reached its all-time peak of 7.2 million metric tons in 1952 during the Korean War. Thereafter, as demand declined and prices fell, production controls were applied. During the remaining pre-revolutionary years, the harvest fluctuated between 4.5 and 5.8 million tons, depending mainly on the state of the world market.

In order to understand what has happened since the Revolution, it is necessary to bear in mind certain elementary facts about sugar as an agricultural crop.

First, cane is a perennial grass which deteriorates in quality unless tended (weeded, fertilized, irrigated, etc.) but which can be cut or left standing from one year to the next for a considerable number of years. In the period of production controls, the area in cane was normally a good deal larger than the area cut. There was therefore a considerable reserve on hand when the Revolution took over, and this was one reason why sugar production could be sharply raised in the first three years. Second, the labor shortage in agriculture did not begin to make itself felt until the 1962 crop. And third, these first three years of the Revolution were all years of ample rainfall, as can be seen from Chart 1.

Cuba's climate is characterized by two seasons: the rainy

Chart 1
Nationwide Average
Yearly Rainfall
(twelve-month period ending April 30)

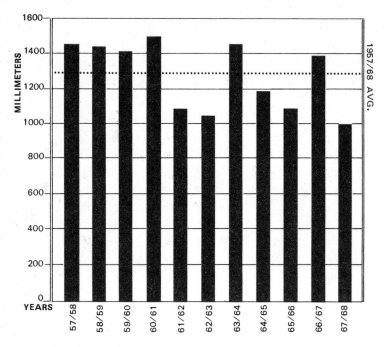

*Source: Granma,* June 30, 1968.

hot season, May through October; and the dry cooler season,
November through April. This climatological pattern deter-
mines the cycle of sugar production. The cane grows during
the wet season and matures as the rains let up and the
temperature moderates. It is then cut during the dry season,
during which new plantings and cultivation of the sprouts
from retained old plantings (called ratoon cane) must also be
carried out. A shortage of rainfall, if severe, can cause the

cane to wither, but it is more usual for drought to manifest itself in a reduced sugar content per stalk. As a result, a poor harvest may require almost as much labor, transportation, and milling as a good harvest. If we go by calendar years, the amount and distribution of rainfall in one year (mostly in the May-November period) will be reflected in the harvest of the next year (January to June). If, as in Chart 1, the year is measured from May 1 to April 30 and listed as 1957/58, 1958/59, etc., the pattern of rainfall will normally be reflected in the harvest of the second of the two years designated.

With this as background, let us look at the record of sugar production since the Revolution took over (Table 8).

Table 8
Cuban Sugar Production
(millions of metric tons)

| | |
|---|---|
| 1959 | 6.0 |
| 1960 | 5.9 |
| 1961 | 6.8 |
| 1962 | 4.8 |
| 1963 | 3.8 |
| 1964 | 4.4 |
| 1965 | 6.1 |
| 1966 | 4.5 |
| 1967 | 6.1 |
| 1968 | 5.1 *(est.)* |

Source: 1959-1967: Junta Central de Planificación (courtesy of the Cuban Mission to the UN). 1968: latest estimates as reported in *Granma*.

After the first three good years, a precipitous decline set in. The pre-revolutionary reserve had long since been used up, and large tracts of sugar land were being plowed under in favor of other crops. Moreover, both 1961/62 and 1962/63 were years of drought (see Chart 1). Finally, by the 1962 harvest the surplus of agricultural labor from which the seasonal cane-cutters had been traditionally recruited had been replaced by a shortage.

In 1964, the results of the new development strategy began to show. With expanded acreage and good rainfall, that year's crop (4.4 million metric tons) was up from the 1963 low of 3.8 million. And the further advance to 6.1 million tons in 1965 seemed to suggest that sugar production had really taken off and was well on its way to the target of ten million tons by 1970. What was particularly impressive about the 1965 performance was that a 30 percent increase in the sugar harvest came in a year (1964/65) of drought: rainfall was down 18 percent as compared to 1963/64 and was well under the 1957-1968 average.

If we look more closely, however, we see that this association of a rise in sugar production with a decline in rainfall is more apparent than real. Monthly figures show that rainfall was actually above average during the crucial May-November period when the 1965 crop was growing and maturing.[1] The real drought began in December, 1964, too late to have much influence on the 1965 crop. But from then through January, 1966, rainfall was below average in every single month and the total for the thirteen-month period was 27 percent below the 1957-1968 norm. The full impact of the drought was therefore felt in the 1966 crop which, at 4.5 million tons, fell 25 percent compared to 1965 and was the second lowest crop of the revolutionary period.

But evidence was not long in coming that improved cultivation practices—better choice of cane varieties, closer planting, and above all more intensive fertilization—could reduce the degree of dependence of the sugar crop on the

---

[1] *Granma,* June 30, 1968.

amount of rainfall. The year 1967 showed the usual relationship: rainfall was excellent in 1966/67 and the crop advanced
to 6.1 million tons, up 24 percent over 1966. The test came
with this year's (1968) crop. In terms of the island as a
whole, 1967/68 was the driest year of the revolutionary
period and the fourth driest of the twentieth century. And
even these overall data greatly understate the extent of the
disaster. The three easternmost provinces (Oriente,
Camagüey, and Las Villas) produce about four-fifths of the
total sugar crop, and it was precisely in these provinces that
the drought was concentrated. In his speech of March 13,
1968, Fidel gave the following figures for rainfall by provinces,
to which we have added the respective percentage declines:

Table 9
Rainfall by Provinces
(in millimeters)

|  | 1966 | 1967 | Percent decline |
|---|---|---|---|
| Pinar del Río | 1,558 | 1,348 | 13.4 |
| Havana | 1,651 | 1,242 | 24.8 |
| Matanzas | 1,702 | 1,338 | 21.4 |
| Las Villas | 1,587 | 1,042 | 34.3 |
| Camagüey | 1,468 | 960 | 34.6 |
| Oriente | 1,324 | 837 | 28.5 |

In these circumstances it can only be said that the 1968
harvest of around 5.1 million tons is a pretty good showing.[2]

[2] The 5.1 million figure understates the harvest by perhaps as
much as a hundred thousand tons because of the diversion of cane to
the production of molasses as emergency feed for cattle threatened
with starvation by the drought. See Raúl Castro's May Day speech in
*Granma*, May 12, 1968.

And when it is considered that during this difficult year a lot of work has gone into preparing next year's harvest—particularly intensive fertilizing—it will be seen that there is considerable reason for optimism. The long drought of 1967-1968 broke in May,[3] and if the rainfall holds up even reasonably well during the remainder of the growing season, 1969 should be a good crop year.

Production, however, would still be far short of the ten-million-ton-by-1970 target. Fidel continues to emphasize that this goal has in no way been modified, and he has in fact gone a good way out on a limb promising that it will be reached. In his speech of March 13 at the University of Havana, he said:

> The question of a sugar harvest of ten million tons has become something more than an economic goal; it is something that has been converted into a point of honor for the Revolution; it has become a yardstick by which to judge the capabilities of the Revolution. . . . And if a yardstick is put up to the Revolution, there is no doubt about the Revolution's meeting the mark.

These may sound like rash words, and perhaps they are; but Fidel is not one to speak them lightly. Perhaps, despite all the difficulties and disappointments of the last few years, Cuba will after all reach the ten-million goal on time. We will have more to say about this and related subjects below.

---

[3] As Fidel said in his speech of May 30 inaugurating several water conservation projects in Oriente Province: "And, as we all know, this year started off even drier than last year. During the first few months . . . Las Villas, Camagüey, and Oriente provinces had even less rainfall than in 1967. But the drought seemed to be nearing its end, and during this month of May the rainfall has been magnificent: the weather bodes well for our country."

**FUEL**

In his speech celebrating the ninth anniversary of the victory of the Revolution, delivered in Havana on January 2, 1968, the Prime Minister concentrated his attention on Cuba's increasingly difficult fuel problem. Ever since the United States clamped its economic blockade on Cuba in the summer of 1960, nearly all of the country's oil has come from the Soviet Union.[4] The amount consumed in the last pre-revolutionary year (1958) was 3,012,000 tons and this had risen by 62 percent to 4,867,000 tons by 1967. Castro did not give exact figures for each year, but he did say that there had been virtually no change in the three years 1961-1963 and that thereafter the average annual rate of increase was 5.5 percent. From these data we can deduce that the rate of increase must have been high—on the order of 12 to 15 percent—in 1959 and 1960. It seems likely that with the increasing expansion and mechanization of the Cuban economy, oil requirements will continue to grow at least as fast as they did in the 1964-1968 period. Will Cuba be able to get the oil it needs? In his January 2 speech, Fidel did not hide his concern about this:

It should be stated that the Soviet Union has gone to considerable lengths to provide fuel. (*Applause.*) This effort is seen, for

---

[4] Castro revealed that Cuba's domestic production of oil in 1967 was 113,000 tons, out of a total consumption of nearly five million tons. Considerable drilling is going on in various parts of the country, and a number of successes have been scored, especially in the Guanabo area some twenty miles east of Havana. Further, in his speech of April 19 commemorating the seventh anniversary of Playa Girón, Fidel announced that Cuba had been granted a $30-million credit by Rumania to expand drilling operations. On the whole, the Cuban leaders are optimistic about the future of domestic production, though they recognize that it will hardly play an important role in the next few years.

example, in the arrival of 162 tankers in 1967 — that is, one vessel approximately every 54 hours. But everything points to the fact that that nation's present possibilities of providing fuel at the rising rate of our needs are limited. And we are in full development, at the most decisive point of our economic advance. . . .

The nature of the "limits" on Soviet capacity to supply Cuba is not clear. Certainly not production, since the Soviet Union is now approaching an annual output of 300 million tons of oil [5] and by all accounts has a growing exportable surplus for which she is trying to develop markets, especially in Western Europe. Perhaps there are problems of finding the necessary tanker tonnage, or perhaps the limits are of a more political than technical or economic character. In any case, it is clear that oil is a potential bottleneck for the Cuban economy and that strict economy will have to be practiced in its use in the foreseeable future. This accounts for the measures announced by Fidel in his January 2 speech, most important of which, from the point of view of the public, was the rationing of gasoline for private automobiles. In a later speech, on April 19, Fidel credited to gasoline rationing the fact that all agricultural equipment had kept operating through the peak months of harvesting and planting.

Apart from its economic consequences, gasoline rationing has had an important social impact. Since no cars have been imported for private use since 1959, automobile traffic was on the decline even before gas rationing. Afterward, it dropped sharply. Havana must have less traffic, and consequently less noise and air pollution, than any other major city in the Western Hemisphere. At a strategic intersection where several streets feed into the Malecón (Havana's broad waterfront drive), in a one-minute period we counted eighteen cars going in all directions at what would normally have been

---

[5] *Pravda,* February 6, 1968.

the morning rush hour (several times that number could have, and in the old days would have, been crowded into the area at the same time). And returning to our hotel from Marianao on Fifth Avenue one afternoon at about six o'clock, the driver cruised along at close to 100 kilometers an hour (about 60 mph) without making anyone in the least nervous. The fact is that the private automobile is on the way out in Cuba, at the same time that it is looming ever larger in the economic planning and social life of the socialist countries of Eastern Europe. We have commented elsewhere on what seems to us the disaster of automobilization in the Soviet Union,[6] and we take this opportunity to record the opinion that the process of de-automobilization which is taking place in Cuba, despite many difficulties and inconveniences, will be enormously beneficial in the long run. The private automobile is a great *unequalizer;* and by the same token its abolition in a country which has already reached a relatively advanced stage of automobilization can be regarded as a necessary prerequisite to the development of a reasonably non-stratified life-style for the whole population.

To continue this digression for a moment: Cubans have been too busy with other things to think or plan much about the disappearance of the private automobile, and there are probably many who assume, consciously or unconsciously, that they are now in a passing phase which in due course will be followed by re-automobilization. To us, however, it seems highly probable that this "passing phase" will last many years, even decades, and that long before it becomes possible to reintroduce the private automobile, Cuba may enter a new phase in which it will have no place and will not even be

---

[6] In our contribution to Huberman and Sweezy (eds.), *Fifty Years of Soviet Power* (New York and London: Monthly Review Press, 1968), pp. 14-16.

missed. This will of course require the development of new institutions and habits, in particular a vastly expanded and improved system of public transportation and possibly something like communal provision of bicycles at strategically located parking stations.[7]

One other aspect of gas rationing deserves mention: it has been a blow to the free and black markets. Previously, anyone with a car could drive into the countryside and supplement his rations by buying from private peasants, at prices considerably higher than the state procurement prices. This traffic has been reduced, though by no means eliminated, since the introduction of gas rationing. We shall return to this subject when we discuss the problem of the private sector.

### ELECTRIC POWER

In his January 2 speech on the fuel problem, Fidel remarked that production of electric power "is the fundamental base of development in any country." This is true and it lends a special importance to power production as a general indicator of the rate of progress. Fidel gave figures for every year since 1958, to which we have added a column showing each year's percentage increase over the previous year (Table 10).

Here we see a pattern with which we are already familiar: a rapid rate of growth in the first couple of years followed first by a sharp decline in the rate and then a rise and relative stabilization after the adoption of the new development

---

[7] Probably because of its past dependence on, and hence copying of, the United States, there are relatively few bicycles in Cuba and none are produced. Only in the city of Cárdenas, we were told, are bicycles in common use. No one seemed able to explain this exception. When prodded, most of the officials we talked to agreed that Cuba's transportation problems could be eased by greater use of bicycles, but it was apparent that the matter had never been given any serious thought.

Table 10
Electric Power Production, 1958-1967

|  | Millions of kilowatt hours | Percent increase over previous year |
|---|---|---|
| 1958 | 1,795 | — |
| 1959 | 1,993 | 11.1 |
| 1960 | 2,145 | 7.6 |
| 1961 | 2,237 | 4.3 |
| 1962 | 2,258 | 0.9 |
| 1963 | 2,344 | 3.8 |
| 1964 | 2,494 | 6.4 |
| 1965 | 2,592 | 3.9 |
| 1966 | 2,813 | 8.5 |
| 1967 | 3,019 | 7.3 |

strategy and the organizational reforms in 1963-1964. Overall, the increase in power production, 68 percent from 1958 through 1967, is not particularly high for a developing country; but when several large (for Cuba) plants now under construction are finished in the second half of 1968 and 1969, production is scheduled to make a considerable leap forward.

### NICKEL

In Chapter 2 above we referred to our visits to the Nicaro and Moa nickel plants on the north coast of Oriente Province. Situated in the midst of what the Cubans believe to be the largest known nickel ore reserves in the world,[8] both of these

---

[8] In appearance the ore is a deep red earth which is scooped up by huge power shovels. It has a high (40 to 50 percent) iron content which some day, when the refining technology has been perfected and the necessary capital is available, will form the basis of a domestic iron and steel industry.

plants were built and owned by United States corporations. The technology at Nicaro is traditional, but that at Moa is highly modern and complex; and since the plant was still unfinished when the Revolution took over, the Americans didn't think the Cubans would be able to operate it—and of course have done, and continue to do, everything possible to keep them from operating it. At Moa we were told a fascinating story of an attempt to buy a certain crucial replacement part made of a highly heat-resistant metal lined with a special kind of ceramic. The intermediary engaged to make the purchase was not suspect to the Americans. When the part arrived at the Moa plant, the Cuban engineers were delighted. The part looked perfect—length, diameter, everything just right. But when they tried to use it, it would not work. The ceramic was not the right type. What had happened showed the stringency of the blockade. When the order was received by the Freeport Sulphur people who had designed and built the Moa plant, they knew at once that no other plant in the world would need that particular part. They therefore filled the order at the regular price but lined the metal tube with the wrong kind of ceramic, so that when the Cubans tried to use it the result was failure.

Since the lack of this one part threatened to close the whole Moa plant down, the Cubans turned for emergency assistance to the socialist countries. Two teams of researchers, one from Czechoslovakia and one from the Soviet Union, took on the assignment of devising a workable replacement part, and both came up with solutions, the Czechs first and the Russians a month or so later.

But it was mostly by their own ingenuity that the Cubans managed to keep nickel production going and finally to master fully the advanced technology of even the Moa plant. We were told by José Alemany, the young director at Moa who is probably more responsible for this achievement than any other person, that there are still a few items they must get from the socialist countries but that the overwhelming majority of replacement parts can now be produced in their own machine shop.

The record of nickel production, as presented by Fidel in his January 2 speech, is given in Table 11 (percentage change figures added). As can be seen, there have been almost as

Table 11
Nickel Production

|        | Metric tons | Percent change compared to previous year |
|--------|-------------|------------------------------------------|
| 1958   | 18,000      | —                                        |
| 1959   | 17,880      | — 0.1                                    |
| 1960   | 14,520      | —18.8                                    |
| 1961   | 18,120      | +24.8                                    |
| 1962   | 24,900      | +37.4                                    |
| 1963   | 21,630      | —13.1                                    |
| 1964   | 24,060      | +11.2                                    |
| 1965   | 29,134      | +21.1                                    |
| 1966   | 27,854      | — 4.4                                    |
| 1967   | 34,900      | +25.3                                    |

many years of declining as of advancing production, but recently the advances have far outweighed the declines. And in September, 1967, a landmark was passed at Nicaro when for the first time monthly production (1,970 tons) surpassed the previous monthly production record (1,912 tons) set in 1957 when the Americans were still in control.[9]

---

[9] *Granma*, June 23, 1968.

Cuba can sell all the nickel it can produce, and the metal has already surpassed tobacco as the country's second (after sugar) biggest export. The largest customers are the USSR, Czechoslovakia, and China; but France and some other capitalist countries are also buyers.

All of this brings great pain to Washington which, as President Dorticós put it, is "as interested in nickel as in a battle in Vietnam." The United States will not import any steel containing Cuban nickel and in every other way does its best to sabotage sales. But all such efforts have been in vain, and one can even say that for the United States in the long run they have been counter-productive. In mastering its nickel industry and beating the blockade, Cuba has scored a victory which has more than economic consequences. It has acquired valuable experience and, even more important, a sense of self-confidence which will stand it in good stead in the years to come.

### CATTLE

As we pointed out in the last chapter, the new development strategy adopted in 1963-1964 assigned a role to cattle second only to that of sugar. And achievements to date have been quite impressive, though as yet yielding very little in the way of benefits to the consuming public. The first problem was to increase the size of the country's cattle herd, and this necessitated a policy of continuing restraint on slaughter, hence no big increases in meat for consumers. According to Fidel's January 2 speech, the number of cattle stood at 5,776,000 in 1961 and had risen to 7,146,800 by 1967—an increase of 24 percent.

Even more important was the task of improving the quality of the cattle. Traditionally, most Cuban cattle have been of the Zebu breed, tough and well adapted to the climate but bad producers of both meat and milk ("these ill-tempered, angry

animals," Fidel called them in his March 13 speech). To solve
this problem, more than 10,000 pure-bred stud bulls have been
imported, and a nationwide artificial insemination program
has been built up from scratch. Before 1959 there was not a
single artificial insemination expert in Cuba, whereas today
there are over 3,000 (according to Fidel on March 13).

We visited the main artificial insemination station outside
Havana where the best bulls are kept, including a giant Holstein from Canada named Black Velvet, reputed to be Fidel's
current favorite. If most readers are as ignorant of the technique as we were, they may find a slight digression instructive.
The bulls' interest in doing their share is stimulated by putting
them in outdoor stanchions before which a number of presumably most attractive cows are paraded. The bulls are next led
to a frame over which a cow's hide has been draped: the
contraption is not very artful but it seems to be good enough
for the aroused bull who eagerly mounts the frame. Under-
neath is an artificial insemination technician manipulating a
simulated vagina made of rubber and brought to the correct
temperature by a sort of sleeve filled with warm water. At the
end of the rubber vagina is a tube which collects the semen as
the bull ejaculates. The semen is then taken to the laboratory
where it is deposited by means of a medicine dropper into
rows of small holes in what appears to be a slab of dry ice. On
contact, the semen freezes into small tablets, each perhaps
half the size of an aspirin tablet. These tablets are then put
into long-handled vials which are immersed in milk-can-sized
containers of liquid nitrogen. It appears that in this extremely
cold state the semen will keep indefinitely. To become usable
the tablets are dissolved in a solution at room temperature,
whereupon the spermatazoa immediately resume full activity,
a process fascinating to watch under the microscope. It was
also fascinating to learn that the insemination station still has

frozen semen from Rosafé Signet, Cuba's most famous bull before his death; in this way Rosafé Signet continues to do his part in upgrading Cuba's cattle herd. We did not have an opportunity to observe the other half of the operation—the fertilization of the cow—but were given to understand that training, skill, and experience on the part of the insemination expert are important if there is to be a high percentage of success. There are insemination stations at various strategic locations around the island, and the technicians work out of them, servicing free of charge the private cattle owners as well as the State Farms.

The Cuban leaders are extremely optimistic about the results they expect from this ambitious program of genetic improvement. Fidel said in his January 2 speech that in the next thirty-six months—i.e., the three years 1968-1970—half a million F-1 (first generation cross between Zebu and Holstein) cows will begin producing milk. Some of the F-1's under specially favorable conditions have already produced twenty to thirty or even more liters of milk a day,[10] but this is certainly far above the average to be expected from the whole island. One well-informed person we talked to thought that eight liters a day would be a safely conservative average figure for the output of these F-1's. This means that by 1970 milk production may increase by as much as 1.2 billion liters a year. Some idea of what this would mean can be gathered when it is pointed out that total purchases of milk by the state procurement agency in 1967 were only 324 million liters.[11]

---

[10] "Rosafé Signet: A Dairy Project Is Developed," *Granma*, June 16, 1968.

[11] According to Fidel's speech on March 13. Procurement is of course less than production since some milk is consumed on the farm or sold by peasants on the free market. However, it can be taken for granted that if production increased by anything like 1.2 billion liters, most of it would be sold to the state.

As with so many things in Cuba, however, this rosy prospect for the future contrasts sharply with the dismal reality of the present. The new cows are not yet producing a significant quantity of milk, and the severe drought of 1967/68 caused a drastic decline in the output of the old cows (mainly through its withering effect on the natural and artificial pastures which still provide the main food supply for Cuba's cattle). While we were in Cuba (February-March, 1968), the milk ration had to be withdrawn from everyone except children under seven and old people over sixty-five. And in the next month, the supply situation grew rapidly worse. In his May Day speech Raúl Castro presented figures for the province of Camagüey (where he was speaking) which illustrate the seriousness of the crisis (Table 12).

Table 12
Daily Purchases of Milk by the
State Procurement Agency
Camagüey Province

| | |
|---|---|
| March  1 | 126,000 kilograms |
| March 31 | 124,000 |
| April  10 | 114,534 |
| April  29 | 90,387 |

With the ending of the drought in May, the situation undoubtedly began to improve. And with the new cows coming into production, it should continue to improve for a long time to come. That, at any rate, is the hope.

### LAND UNDER CULTIVATION

One of the most obvious and least excusable evils of pre-revolutionary Cuba was the coexistence of huge amounts of uncultivated land on the one hand and desperately poor and chronically unemployed labor on the other. Against this background it is not surprising that from the moment it took power the revolutionary government has been passionately devoted to bringing new land into production. Bulldozers, tractors, even tanks have been used to clear thousands of square miles of scrub and *marabu*. In 1958, according to Fidel's January 2 speech, there were 2,379,103 hectares of land under cultivation; by 1967 this had risen by 56 percent to 3,711,800 hectares. And even now a huge militarized, highly mechanized brigade called the Che Guevara Trailblazers Brigade is hard at work clearing more thousands of hectares. Taken by themselves, these feats of land-clearing are undoubtedly very impressive. Whether they have always reflected the wisest use of available resources is another matter.[12]

EGGS

Without any doubt the most spectacular economic success of the Cuban Revolution has been in the production of eggs. Since this was the field in which the new organizational principles of 1963-1964 were pioneered and where the best results were obtained, it seems worthwhile to quote at length from Michel Gutelman's description of what happened:

The egg combine was a sort of anticipation. It was the product of the intuition which gave rise to the new principles of organization and at the same time preceded the clear formulation of those principles. Set up in 1963 on the personal initiative of Prime Minister Fidel Castro, it taught many lessons.

Up to 1963 the production of eggs was in the hands of numerous State Farms for which it was only one activity among many. This dispersion, combined with the relative powerlessness of the production units, resulted in low production and low productivity. Veritable egg "factories" existed, but absence of coordina-

---

[12] See pp. 169-171 below.

tion with the other branches of the economy was the source of many deficiencies. Supplying of material requirements was subject to the fluctuations of foreign trade: the technical characteristics of imported feed were not adequately respected. Sometimes minerals were lacking, sometimes vitamins or cereals. (The problem was less one of the availability of foreign exchange than of its rational utilization.) Distribution was particularly disorganized: it was subject to sudden interruptions and suffered from all the ills that plagued the Ministry of Internal Commerce and the organization of transportation.

The creation of a combine integrating all the units of production—on the various farms to which they were attached—and new methods of handling and trading in this product changed, in a very short time, the conditions of production and supply. One can even say that the success was very spectacular. In January, 1964, the production of eggs amounted to 13 million units. In January, 1965, it reached 60 million; and in 1966 it frequently surpassed 90 million a month. In periods of heavy laying, production of more than 120 million a month was attained. Not only the quantity increased but also the quality of the packaging (six units to a box) improved and reached international norms. Unit costs of production declined by around 30 percent. Such a success made it possible to discontinue rationing of eggs within a year and even to export eggs in periods of strong supply. In 1965, for the first time, Cuba sold eggs to Italy. . . .[13]

### TRACTORS

The number of tractors in agriculture (all imported, of course) has risen from 9,200 in 1960 to 35,000 in 1967 (according to Fidel's speech of January 2). This enormous increase in the number of tractors has been an important factor in such successes as have been achieved in agriculture; it has also, as we shall see, helped to create some problems.

---

[13] Gutelman, *op. cit.,* pp. 133-134.

### MISCELLANEOUS PRODUCTS

Rather than continue with a recital of statistics relating to individual items, let us conclude this part of our description of revolutionary Cuba's economic achievements by reproducing part of a table entitled "Cuba: Some Industrial Productions" presented in a document prepared for a meeting sponsored by the United Nations in 1967 [14] (Table 13).

### Table 13
### Output of Miscellaneous Products

| Product | Unit | 1963 | 1966 |
|---|---|---|---|
| Leather footwear | million pairs | 11.8 | 12.6 |
| Detergents | thousand metric tons | 12.9 | 14.3 |
| Beer | million liters | 89.3 | 99.2 |
| Refined vegetable oil | thousand metric tons | 32.1 | 45.8 |
| Powdered milk | thousand metric tons | 49.4 | 61.3 |
| Pasteurized and natural milk | thousand metric tons | 147.1 | 325.1 |
| Butter | thousand metric tons | 2.2 | 2.7 |
| Bread and biscuits | thousand metric tons | 153.5 | 376.1 |
| Flour products | thousand metric tons | 22.3 | 33.9 |
| Cigarettes | million units | 15.3 | 18.4 |
| Cotton products | million square meters | 60.4 | 92.0 |

These are all items of mass consumption, and the average increase for the three-year period works out to just over 45 percent.

This looks like a good record, and in a way it certainly is. On the other hand, it should not be allowed to give rise to any

[14] *Industrial Development in Cuba: Report Presented by the Cuban Delegation to the International Symposium on Industrial Development.* 1967 (mimeographed).

illusions that consumer needs are close to being met. For one thing, though we have no comparable data for later periods, there is reason to believe that since 1966 consumption has been further squeezed in favor of exports and investments. Nearly everyone we talked to agreed that shortages had grown worse in the last year, and Fidel in his January 2 speech stated quite frankly that 1968 would "be considered as one of the rough years of the Revolution." Apart from the effects of the drought—by no means confined to sugar and cattle, the two areas discussed above—an important part of the explanation was given by Fidel in his March 13 speech when he presented figures on state investments. In 1967, he said, the total figure was 979 million pesos (officially 1 peso = 1 dollar) which was 27.1 percent of the "available gross national product"—a very high percentage by any standards. But the estimate for 1968 he put at no less than 1,240 million pesos, up 26.7 percent in a single year and 31 percent of the estimated gross national product![15] "We believe," he added, "that no other underdeveloped country today is making anything even remotely—not even remotely—like this kind of effort." This is very likely true; and since what is invested cannot be consumed, it goes far to explain the extreme austerity of life in Cuba today, so much commented on by all visitors to the island.

Before we leave this subject, however, we must emphasize that Cuban austerity is not like that in the underdeveloped countries of the "free world." In the latter the burden of austerity is borne by the workers, peasants, unemployed, etc., whose incomes are extremely low or nonexistent and who usually make up from 75 to 90 percent of the population. The middle strata live in relative comfort and the ruling oligarchies

---

[15] Fidel also gave the following investment figures for earlier years (all in millions of pesos); 1962: 607.6; 1963: 716.8; 1964: 794.9; 1965: 827.1; 1966: 909.8.

in outrageous luxury. The shops are full only because the price-income system keeps the vast majority from buying what is in them. To the superficial observer there appear to be no shortages; to most of the people there are nothing but shortages. How right the Cuban boy was who said to José Yglesias: "If everyone in Mexico could afford to buy a pair of shoes, how many do you think would be left in the stores?"[16]

The point is that in Cuba everyone *can* afford to buy a pair of shoes, and there are never any left in the stores. And the same goes for nearly all other consumer goods. The explanation is twofold: First, the minimum wage in Cuba is 85 pesos a month and a large percentage of workers get two or three times as much. Moreover, there is a labor shortage so that every able-bodied person can get a job and many families have two or more wage earners. Second, average rents are very low, education and health and some other services are free, and rationed goods are cheap. The result is a large volume of "free" purchasing power chasing after a very limited supply of goods. In these circumstances, the shortages which are hidden in other countries rise to the surface for all to see. What's more, they affect the entire population including the top management and the middle strata who would be comfortably off in other countries. In other words, *everyone* feels the shortages, and this sometimes gives the impression that they are a lot worse than they really are.

For the truth is that the shortages which all Cubans have to bear are not nearly as bad as those which afflict the great majority of Latin Americans. On this point, and also on the way the revolutionary government hopes to overcome the shortages, the industrial development report cited is accurate and instructive. Discussing what it calls "disequilibrium be-

---

[16] José Yglesias, *In the Fist of the Revolution* (New York: Pantheon Books, Inc., 1968), p. 102.

tween supply and demand for consumer goods," the report says:

The foundation of this disequilibrium is . . . the rapid increase in the level of monetary incomes of the majority of the population and the lack of capacity for satisfying this new demand through an accelerated rate of domestic production.

The result has been the necessity of establishing rationing of several types and degrees.

It is certain that the level of availability of goods in the rationed categories is higher than average consumption in the majority of Latin American countries and much greater when one speaks in terms of the worker and peasant populations of those countries. But this comparison is not sufficient for a revolution with socialist objectives. Much less is it our intention to eliminate the disequilibrium through retail price methods.

The only acceptable way out—and it is the way that has been chosen by the Cuban Revolution—is the most rapid increase possible of supply until this is adequate to the income of the population, and, finally, to bring about constant additional increases in the standard of living.[17]

Many of the problems which we discuss in subsequent chapters relate precisely to the ways and means of accomplishing these goals.

---

[17] *Industrial Development in Cuba, op. cit.,* pp. 28-29.

# 7

# The Private Sector

For all practical purposes it can be said that when the Revolution came to power the whole Cuban economy was in the private sector. Its size has been progressively reduced and the state sector correspondingly increased in successive stages which, for present purposes, we need only briefly summarize.

### RECOVERY OF ILL-GOTTEN GOODS

In the course of Batista's rule, the dictator and his henchmen had built up large fortunes through force, fraud, and corruption. Partly these took the form of foreign bank accounts and other assets which the revolutionary government could not reach, but there were also estates, factories, etc., inside Cuba, and these the government seized. Similarly, the property of refugees leaving the country has been taken over, a process which began with the triumph of the Revolution and has been going on ever since. In this way the government has acquired most of the housing which belonged to the former upper class (much of it today used to accommodate scholarship students).

## THE FIRST AGRARIAN REFORM

The Agrarian Reform Law of May 17, 1959, laid the foundations of both the private and state sectors in agriculture as we know them today. With certain exceptions, landholdings in excess of thirty *caballerías* (approximately a thousand acres) were confiscated. Part of the land thus acquired was given outright to renters, sharecroppers, and some landless peasants: these small farmers, organized in the *Asociación Nacional de Pequeños Agricultores* (ANAP), constitute the bulk of today's private sector in agriculture. The original intention was that the remainder of the confiscated land would be cultivated by cooperatives. But the cooperative idea never took hold, and what in fact emerged were State Farms.

It is impossible to give precise quantitative figures on the effects of the Agrarian Reform of 1959 because its implementation overlapped with two other measures which also affected the pattern of land ownership. The first was the law of July 6, 1960, passed in retaliation for the abolition of the United States sugar quota. This took over all U.S.-owned properties in agriculture as well as in other branches of the economy. And the second was the law of October 13, 1960, which nationalized all large private enterprises, including Cuban-owned sugar mills, together with the cane lands belonging to the same owners (individuals or corporations). When all these measures had been carried out, the private sector in agriculture had the structure shown in Table 14.

## THE SECOND AGRARIAN REFORM

As will be seen from Table 14, even after all the reforms of 1959-1960, Cuban agriculture was still characterized by a markedly unequal division of land. Relatively large holdings of more than 67 hectares (165 acres), though only 7 percent of the total number of farms, accounted for 47 percent

Table 14
The Private Sector in 1961

| Size of Farms | Number of Farms | Thousands of Hectares |
|---|---|---|
| Up to 67 hectares[a] | 154,703 | 2,348.1 |
| 67 to 134 hectares | 6,062 | 607.5 |
| 134 to 268 hectares | 3,105 | 610.3 |
| 268 to 402 hectares | 1,457 | 507.6 |
| Over 402 hectares | 592 | 377.5 |
| *Total* | 165,919 | 4,451.0 |

[a] 1 hectare = 2.47 acres
Source: *Panorama Económica Latinoamericano*, No. 221, Havana, 1967.

of the privately owned land. And since the private sector at that time included about 56 percent of all agricultural land,[1] it can be seen that over a quarter of the countryside was in the grip of a small stratum of large farmers—some eleven thousand in all who, together with their families, constituted well under 1 percent of the island's total population.

This was a rural bourgeoisie in the full sense of the term and, as was to be expected, it was in its great majority hostile to the Revolution. This hostility was manifested in many ways: through spreading rumors and pessimism in the countryside, through sabotaging production directly or by allowing farms to run down preparatory to leaving the country, but above all through providing a social base for the counterrevolutionary guerrilla bands recruited largely among exiles and armed by the CIA. The Escambray mountains in southern Las Villas Province were the scene of particularly

---

[1] Gutelman, *op. cit.*, p. 58.

heavy fighting in the early 1960's, and the possibility of a new and bigger Bay of Pigs invasion was always present. Under these circumstances, the revolutionary government, following its well-established pattern of taking the initiative against its enemies, decided to liquidate the counterrevolutionary rural bourgeoisie. The result was the Second Agrarian Reform of October 13, 1963, which confiscated all holdings in excess of 67 hectares. After this, according to figures presented by Gutelman, the private sector contained some 3.6 million hectares (39 percent of the total) and the state sector 5.5 million hectares (61 percent of the total).[2]

### THE ROLE OF THE PRIVATE SECTOR IN AGRICULTURE

Since 1963 there has been a gradual and slow shift in the balance between the private and state sectors in favor of the latter. According to the Cuban document presented to the FAO meeting in Rome in 1967, the distribution of land between the two in 1966 was: state sector: 65 percent; private sector: 35 percent.[3] The latter was composed of about 200,000 production units ranging up to 67 hectares in size. Classified by their main products, these private farms are distributed as shown in Table 15.

As can be seen, the private sector is by no means specialized to one or a few crops but plays a role in all the main branches of Cuban agriculture. Its relative importance in the overall

---

[2] *Ibid.*, p. 58. Gutelman notes that while the "fundamental and official" reasons for the Second Agrarian Reform were political in nature, nevertheless the measure "was also undoubtedly motivated by purely technical considerations in that it permitted a regrouping of state units which up to that time had been very dispersed and divided into small parcels."

[3] *Agricultural and Livestock Production in Cuba, 1965-1967*, p. 154. The material in this and the next two paragraphs is taken from this source (pp. 154-155).

Table 15
Private Farms by Main Products
(in percentages)

| | |
|---|---|
| Tobacco | 17.6 |
| Sugar cane | 17.1 |
| Cattle | 16.1 |
| Root vegetables | 15.4 |
| Coffee | 13.9 |
| Cereals | 10.5 |
| Other | 9.4 |
| *Total* | 100.00 |

*Source:* See note 3.

Table 16
Percentages of State Purchases
of Various Crops Coming from
Private Farms in 1966

| | |
|---|---|
| All crops[a] | 36 |
| Sugar | 32 |
| Meat | 20 |
| Milk | 40 |
| Root vegetables[b] | 58 |
| Garden vegetables[c] | 69 |
| Fruit | 69 |
| Coffee | 83 |
| Tobacco | 90 |
| Cocoa | 95 |

[a] 1965
[b] Including plantains
[c] Including pumpkins
*Source:* See note 3.

agricultural picture can be better understood in terms of the percentages of total purchases of main crops by state procurement agencies accounted for by private farms (Table 16).

Since 1965 there has been a tendency for these procurement percentages to decline both because of the slow shrinkage of the private sector and because the major investment effort in agriculture has been and continues to be in the state sector. Nevertheless, the importance of the private sector in the economy as a whole is considerably greater than the procurement data indicate. This is because a large but unrecorded share of the production of private farms is either consumed directly by the farmers and their families or is sold on the free market. (We were told that in the case of some crops no more than 30 percent of the output of the private sector is sold to the state.)

### CONTRADICTIONS INHERENT IN THE PRIVATE SECTOR

There is no doubt that along with the rural and urban proletariats, the small peasantry of the private sector has from the outset been one of the indispensable pillars of the Revolution. The liquidation of the rural bourgeoisie through the Second Agrarian Reform was relatively easy because it had the backing of the small peasants, and the almost total absence of counterrevolutionary activity in the countryside since 1963 is attributable to the same basic cause. No one knows better than Fidel Castro that substantial disaffection among the small peasantry would disrupt the class alliance which up to now has given the revolutionary regime its unshakable strength and stability. And no one has been more explicit or more unequivocal in assuring and reassuring the small peasants that the Second Agrarian Reform was the last and that thenceforth their status would be fully respected. At that time he stated the policy of the revolutionary government in the following words: "We can definitely state that the small landowners will cultivate their land as they see fit, either as individual farmers, as individual members of the Credit and Service Cooperatives, or as members of the Agricultural Societies, just as they wish or prefer."[5] And in later years the same pledge has been repeated on many occasions and in many formulations. It is probably not an exaggeration to say that no policy of the revolutionary government is more firmly established.

From the short-run economic point of view, as well as from the political point of view, the existence of the private sector may well be considered an important asset and stabilizing factor. Not only do the small peasants produce a large part of their own food but also through their sales on the free market they provide an important supplement to the supplies reaching consumers through state channels. We shall return to the subject of the free market presently; for the moment we note only that the evidence we were able to collect was enough to convince us that for the country as a whole and on the average, the food situation is considerably better than one is led to believe either by official statistics or by people one meets in Havana. Not only in the countryside itself but also in small towns and even in provincial capitals, consumers have, and take advantage of, opportunities to buy directly from private peasants. And this is perhaps the decisive factor in localizing discontent largely in the capital (another subject to which we shall return in due course).

The positive aspects of the existence of a private sector in agriculture, then, are (1) that the small peasant who owes practically everything he has to the Revolution remains a staunch supporter of the revolutionary regime so long as it continues to uphold his interests; and (2) that the output of the private sector provides not only an important part of

---

[5] *Ibid.*, p. 153.

state agricultural procurements but also, through auto-consumption and the free market, a stabilizing supplement to what consumers are able to buy through official outlets. But there are also negative aspects which in our view, and we believe in the view of the Cuban leaders, a socialist country can neglect only at its peril. One of these, the inherent technological backwardness of small peasant farming, is universally recognized, has been repeatedly stressed by the Cubans,[6] and calls for no elaboration here.

The second major negative aspect is less recognized, or at any rate less talked about, but in our view no less important. We refer to the corrosive and corrupting effect, both socially and morally, of private enterprise as such. The small peasants support the Revolution because it has brought them great benefits, but it does not follow that they are revolutionaries or that as a class they can ever be expected to be revolutionaries. On the contrary, they are petty bourgeois with all the spiritual traits and mental habits of the petty bourgeoisie: orientation toward the market and money, selfishness, graspingness, parochialism, low cultural level, cynicism. And the objective situation in Cuba is such that they not only have the freedom and opportunity to act in accordance with their (socially conditioned) nature but also to enrich themselves in the process.

Naturally when we say "enrich" we are not thinking in terms of capitalist millionaires, nor are we suggesting that there are not poor, indeed desperately poor, small peasants. But we think the term is appropriate and refers to a very real

---

[6] See, for example, Fidel's speech of January 6, 1968, inaugurating a village of new homes in the Havana Green Belt. This speech also contains as explicit a discussion as we have seen of what the government sees as the long-run solution of the small peasant problem. We quote from it extensively below, pp. 125-128.

if too much neglected phenomenon. To understand this, one must bear in mind that the 165-acre limitation on the size of private farms allows what in many countries would be considered large-scale agricultural enterprises. And when it is considered that many of these larger farms are on the best lands, it will be appreciated that what the Cubans call "small" peasants may in fact resemble what we in the United States would call operators of prosperous family-sized farms.

So far as we know, there is very little published material on the structure, functioning, income, etc., of the private peasant sector, but we did pick up here and there from conversations and discussions bits of information which throw some light on the nature of the problems involved. For example:

• While private individuals own only 30 percent of all land on the island, their share of arable land (i.e., of *good* land) is 43 percent.[7]

• Private farmers with incomes of ten, fifteen, or even twenty thousand pesos a year are not uncommon. This compares with cabinet ministers' incomes of 700 pesos a month (8400 a year) and a high for technicians and other specialists in industry of around ten thousand a year. It is thus safe to say that in the economically active population, apart from a few remaining physicians still in private practice, the richest people in Cuba today are private farmers.

• The private sector employs, in addition to the labor of the owners and their families, nearly 60,000 workers. This indicates the continued existence on a not inconsiderable scale of capitalist relations in the countryside. The status of these hired workers is not clear to us, but we got the impression that

---

[7] These figures are not strictly comparable to those presented earlier on the relative sizes of the state and private sectors in agriculture, presumably because these include—and the earlier ones did not— lands not suitable for agricultural use.

THE PRIVATE SECTOR   119

at least some are State Farm employees doubling as hired hands for private farmers. Most if not all of this private employment is illegal but is apparently tolerated for a combination of political and economic reasons (suppression would involve police-state methods, would be unpopular with both employers and employees, and would cause considerable disruption of production).

How is it possible for private farmers, or at least a stratum of private farmers, to do so well economically under a socialist regime?

Basically, the answer is that the state needs their support and *wants* them to do well. It therefore pays prices for their products which are remunerative for the better managed farms and agrees to take all they can produce. And it permits the smaller and less specialized farms to sell their vegetables, chicken, milk, fruit, etc., on the free market at several times the official price.[8]

To avoid misunderstanding: we do not criticize the revolutionary regime for these policies toward the private sector in agriculture. We have no doubt that—apart perhaps from details, which we are in no position to evaluate—they are wise and necessary. But we also think it is desirable to discuss their consequences and in particular not to obscure the high cost a socialist society has to pay to maintain the loyalty of a petty bourgeoisie it cannot afford to antagonize and is not yet strong enough to absorb into the socialist system.

---

[8] José Yglesias, who spent several months during the first half of 1967 in Mayarí on the north coast of Oriente, quotes a retired worker to the effect that "prices at the government stores were more or less what they had been before the Revolution, but the campesinos usually sold their chickens and vegetables at three times that. (*In the Fist of the Revolution,* p. 139.) This would indicate an even bigger spread between the government's procurement prices and free market prices. We have no way of judging the accuracy or representativeness of this information.

Part of that cost is economic, the preservation of an essentially backward mode of production on a large part of the country's good agricultural land. As long as the state sector is also underdeveloped and characterized by low productivity, however, this may not be too serious. What is undoubtedly serious is the social and moral cost of having a segment of the population amounting to 10 percent or more of the total (200,000 private proprietors plus families and dependents) as permanent "carriers" of a petty bourgeois mentality and outlook.

Even this would perhaps not matter too much if this segment of the population were isolated from the remainder, living its own life and stewing in its own juice. But of course this is not the way it is in reality. There are close and continuing relations between the private peasantry and the rest of the population both in the ordinary course of social existence and more specifically through the free market. Thus, the private peasantry stands in the very midst of socialist society as a generator of bourgeois ideas and values and consequently as a focus of infection to which few of the other strata of society can as yet be considered immune. It is in any case extremely difficult for a people who have been subjected for centuries to the horrors and barbarities of exploitation and class rule to learn and absorb the new values and attitudes without which there is no chance of the flourishing of socialism and communism. This difficulty is multiplied if at the same time all the crippling effects of colonial underdevelopment must be overcome. And it is even further compounded if a substantial part of the population, because of its immersion in the old mode of production, not only cannot participate in the process of liberation but on the contrary must act as an obstacle in its path.

Cuba today unfortunately—and unavoidably—labors under all these disadvantages.

THE FUTURE OF THE PRIVATE SECTOR IN AGRICULTURE

The revolutionary leadership knows as well as anyone else that the only solution to the problem of the private sector in agriculture is to abolish it. But it also knows that this cannot be accomplished by fiat and that the process will necessarily be a prolonged one. It has therefore devised a strategy which, at the risk of overschematization, can be summed up under the three headings of "containment," "attrition," and "abundance." These are closely interrelated, particularly the last two, but can most conveniently be discussed separately.

*Containment.* The major objective here is to restrict the scope and profitability of the free market as much as possible without actually clamping controls on the peasants' activities. This is accomplished mainly by making it difficult for buyers and sellers to get together. There is no free market in the sense of a marketplace where peasants can bring, display, and sell their wares, such as exists in the Soviet Union and at least some other socialist countries. Buyers must seek out sellers, and there is a limit of twenty-five pounds on the amount a buyer may bring back with him. The main burden of violations thus falls on the consumer, not on the producer—which is in accord with the government's policy of not antagonizing the private peasants. There are also certain other regulations relating to these transactions, and all of them taken together define what is legal and what illegal.[9] The black market, as distinct from the free market, comprises transactions which exceed the legal limits, plus of course traffic in goods which are

---

[9] It might be more accurate to say "What is tolerated and what is not tolerated." President Dorticós, in describing agricultural policy to us, remarked that private trade to consumers is illegal but that it is not repressed by police methods. It is a nice question whether activities prohibited by laws which are not enforced are legal or illegal. In any case, for purposes of a popular exposition it seems preferable to reserve the term "illegal" for activities which are subject to concrete sanctions.

illegally diverted from the state sector. A typical black market operation, for example, would be the purchase by a consumer of a 100-pound bag of rice from a private farmer.[10]

Given this set-up, it is easy to see why gasoline rationing was a blow to the free and black markets.[11] Before rationing it was easy for anyone with a car (or access to a car) and established relations with one or more small farmers to go to the countryside at will and bring back food, twenty-five pounds on each trip without fear of interference. But since rationing of gas has been instituted, such mobility has been greatly restricted; and of course shopping in the countryside by bus or on foot is an entirely different matter.

In summary, one can say that the government's policy has been to discourage rather than prevent trade between the private peasantry and the consuming public. In the nature of the case there is no way to measure the results of this policy in quantitative terms; but one can certainly say that if the opposite policy of encouraging and institutionalizing the free market had been adopted, as many socialist countries have done, the demand for the products of the private sector would have been higher, the profits of this trade and hence the resources devoted to it would have been larger, and the power and influence of the private sector would have been enhanced. In this sense, then, the policy of "containment" has undoubtedly been successful.

*Attrition.* Privately owned land can pass by inheritance from parents to children but it cannot be sold except to the state. There will thus always be a certain amount of land being transferred from the private sector to the public sector

---

[10] This example was actually cited to us. The price would be about 250 pesos, and the most likely buyer would be one of the physicians who are still in private practice.

[11] See above, p. 96.

as owners die without children, and a certain amount more as owners wishing to retire and children inheriting land but not wishing to cultivate it sell to the state.

The revolutionary government expects that this process of attrition will speed up as time goes by. It believes that sons and daughters of peasants, given increasing opportunities for technical and higher education and with an unlimited number of careers in industry, modernized collective agriculture, and public service opening up to them, will become less and less interested in following in the footsteps of their parents and will sell or cede their land to the state as they acquire title to it. There is already evidence that this is happening and little reason to doubt that it will continue to happen in the future—provided, of course, that the more attractive openings in the socialist sectors of the economy materialize as planned and expected.

But attrition, however effective it may promise to be in the long run, is necessarily a slow process, and the revolutionary leaders do not feel that they can afford to wait for an indefinite period while an important part of the country's agriculture remains in a state of backwardness and low productivity. They are therefore adopting additional policies toward the private sector which aim to make it contribute to the creation of an abundance which they hope will undermine its own continued existence.

*Abundance.* If we understand correctly what the Cubans are saying, the underlying theory here may be summed up as follows: At the present time there is a great scarcity of consumer goods relative to money demand. After people buy what they can from state stores at low official prices, they have money left over with which they can bid up prices on the free and black markets. As supplies become more abundant, they will be able to satisfy more of their needs at the low-price stores, and prices on the private markets will decline until eventually the gap is eliminated. At this point the private markets will disappear along with their *raison d'être*, which was the scarcity of goods at the regular stores.

This happy event is still a long way off, and it is perhaps not very important at this stage to inquire what will happen thereafter. Still, it is not without interest to show that the theory can be logically extended to encompass the disappearance of the private sector itself. All we need do is assume that the modernization and technification of the state sector result in a more rapid increase of productivity there than in the private sector (President Dorticós was emphatic in telling us that this is already happening). If prices are held constant, the state sector will then yield a growing surplus, part of which can be used to raise the material and cultural standards of the State Farm workers more rapidly than those of the private peasants. Increasingly, therefore, the latter will find it advantageous to transfer from the private to the public sector —a new form of the attrition process described above. An item in the *New York Times* of August 1, 1968, datelined Miami, suggests that such transfers are already under way:

> Cuban peasants are "ceding" their land to the state, the Havana radio reported today. It said that more than 1,100 acres in Pinar del Río province formerly owned by 43 small farmers had recently been incorporated into the region's state farms.
>
> The cession of farms, the Havana radio added, was made by peasants "conscious that with it production will increase and that they are advancing the construction of a new socialist society."
>
> Although reported only briefly and sporadically, transfers of land to the state appear to be part of a larger governmental plan to reduce private property in Cuban agriculture to a minimum.

Our guess would be that the small peasants are motivated

less by social consciousness than by a desire to improve their condition, and that the brief and sporadic reporting of such transfers reflects the fact that they are as yet of minor importance and that for the present the focus of the government's policy toward the small peasant is quite different. What the government is trying to do, in fact, is to raise the productivity of small peasants and bring them into the framework of the state planning system while respecting their status as private owners. The pioneer project in this connection is the Havana Green Belt, and the chief instrument is the so-called microplan whereby the individual peasant agrees to conform his production to the general plan in exchange for certain kinds of help from the state. In his speech of January 6, 1968, Fidel explained these matters in considerable detail, having in mind that his audience contained many foreign guests who had come to Cuba to attend the Cultural Congress. It will be useful to quote at some length:

The Green Belt was begun on April 17, 1967, and it should be completed in 1968. It provides for agricultural development of the area around the capital city, and includes housing for the workers and farmers of the whole region. Part of this area is state owned and part is owned by small farmers. The program calls for full development of the zone, including housing and the necessary agricultural installations.

Already 458 houses have been built, as well as 130 small pigpens, 100 hen houses, 79 barns, 338 other buildings—dining halls, storehouses—and 280 landscaping projects.

The Green Belt includes approximately 2,300 *caballerías* of land. For Europeans and guests from other countries that do not use *caballerías* as a unit of measurement, one *caballería* is 13.4 hectares [33.2 acres]. So an area of 2,300 *caballerías* is approximately 30,000 hectares. Of these 30,000 hectares, about 19,000 will be planted to fruit trees, with coffee interplanted.

The rest of the area includes some six or seven thousand

hectares of pasturelands, slightly farther out, and two woodland parks. . . . There will also be botanical gardens, extending over 500 hectares, which will be under the University of Havana School of Botany. In addition, there will be a new zoo for the city of Havana. . . .

Other areas will be used for reservoirs, now under construction. The 2,300 *caballerías* or 30,000 hectares of the Green Belt will be irrigated. . . .

And so, in this province, we have begun a new policy, directed toward the rational and optimum use of all lands — state as well as privately owned. And since we have the advantage of beginning with a very low degree of productivity from these privately owned lands, this permits us to rationalize the use of such lands in such a way that both the farmer and the nation benefit.

In the first place, all investments are made by the state. That means that if we have to break new ground, if we have to create a new plantation, including the productive installations, we include housing in such plans, and we do not apply a mercantile policy. The farmer does not have to get involved, does not have to go one cent into debt to the state. Thus we develop that unit of production, and the ultimate responsibility of the farmer is simply to care for it, using adequate technical methods, and derive the maximum yield from it. If it is a crop that calls for additional effort, we mobilize the nation's labor force and bring in the harvests just as on the plantations. And in this way these tremendous projects you have seen around Havana are being carried out.

In the final analysis, by taking full advantage of these lands, we are going to create such an abundance of those products that in the not too distant future the products involved in these plans will also be withdrawn from mercantile circulation. So that society cultivates the state lands and invests in the lands that do not belong to the state; it makes investments, contributes to their development, contributes to their exploitation in order to create a productivity that will permit the country to practically withdraw all those products from mercantile circulation. That is, our society is seriously dedicated to moving toward communist distribution. *(Applause.)*

Naturally, this must be based on the maximum development of technology, labor productivity, and productivity of the land.

Immediately, all of the farm population that receives the benefit of these small-scale plans [microplans], improves its situation tremendously. Thus, incomparably better living and working conditions are created, as in these present cases, for many who lived before in huts that were practically detrimental to health.

And to have an idea of what this plan means economically — for example, here in Havana's Green Belt — suffice it to say that the value of what is produced per hectare will increase twenty times. That is, once it is in production, each hectare of these lands that we are working will be producing economic values twenty times greater than it was producing before . . . .

In other words, a real revolution in agriculture is being carried out in this province just as in the rest of the country.

How have the farmers received these plans? Naturally, they have received them with extraordinary enthusiasm, with extraordinary optimism, with extraordinary joy.

Thus the contradiction that existed between that private ownership of the land and the low productivity of this land, on the one hand, and the interests of society, on the other, has been resolved, has been overcome, in the only way that interests us, and in the way that we must overcome any contradiction in the heart of our revolutionary society—that is, within the masses of the workers and farmers; any contradiction whatever.

And in truth one of the most difficult problems in revolutionary processes has been the agrarian question of the small farmer. . . .

How did the small-scale plans begin? The small-scale plans began with some farmers. And others asked what those small-scale plans were. Little by little, as the plans acquired prestige, more and more farmers wanted to join them. So much so that the vast majority of the farmers in the Havana Green Belt—I would say more than 90 percent—have joined the plans. What is happening in each and every region of the country is that the farmers are asking when the small-scale plans will come to their region, when the small-scale plans will come to their province. That is the problem. Unfortunately, we can't carry them out at the rate they want them or that we do, either.

It is no wonder that the small peasants welcome the coming of these microplans since the effect is to relieve them of all the normal financial and business responsibilities of the private owner while guaranteeing their incomes. On the one hand, apart from the peasant's own labor, inputs (machine services, fertilizers, pesticides, even volunteer labor to bring in the harvest) are provided free of charge by the state; on the other hand, the owner gets paid for what is grown on his land in the regular way. On the production side, in other words, his position is hardly distinguishable from that of a worker on a state farm, while on the income side he continues to be paid both for his labor and his land.

It may be, as Fidel predicts, that the increased productivity made possible by rationalizing the use of the small peasants' land and labor will be such that both society as a whole and the small private producers will benefit from this arrangement. If so, it will contribute to creating the abundance which will narrow and eventually eliminate the gap between official and free market prices. Whether it will also hasten the decline of the private sector in agriculture, however, is another matter. Since the small peasants are to share in the increased product not only as workers but also as owners, it could be argued that the generalization of the microplans will confer further benefits on what is already in some ways a privileged class and thus create new vested interests which the members of the class will be reluctant to give up.

The number of variables at work here is too great and our knowledge of them much too limited to permit us to speak with any assurance about these matters. But we believe we can say that, on the evidence available to us, the problem of the private sector in agriculture which Fidel, in the speech quoted above, correctly termed "one of the most difficult problems in revolutionary processes" is still far from solved and will continue to plague the revolutionary leadership for a long time to come.

Before we leave this subject, a word about Fidel's references to withdrawing products from mercantile circulation, which he identifies with communist distribution. "Mercantile circulation" presumably means the exchange of goods against money (goods which are produced with a view to such exchange are called commodities or, in Spanish, *mercancías*). Goods withdrawn from mercantile circulation are therefore no longer exchanged against money and cease to be commodities. There are of course various other possibilities: for example the total available quantity of each type of goods might be divided by the total population and each person might be given his or her aliquot share. But since Fidel speaks of communist distribution, we must assume that what he has in mind is not a system of this kind but rather free distribution "to each according to his needs."

With nearly everything desperately scarce in Cuba today, it might appear that it is foolishness, or worse, to talk about free distribution of anything according to need. We do not agree with this, however. To begin with, we believe that it is the responsibility, indeed duty, of serious communists not to relegate communist goals to a sort of sacred literature which deals with a faraway paradise on earth, much as the literature of Christianity deals with heaven and hell. Communist goals and ideals, if they have any purpose other than to deceive the gullible, must play a part in the concrete planning and action of the here and now. That Fidel understands this and in his speeches, which are above all the discourses of a master teacher, seeks always to relate the revolutionary government's policies to the attainment of communist goals, seems to us to be not a weakness but on the contrary a measure of his greatness as a revolutionary and a communist.

But, it may be said, to talk about communist goals in the present state of scarcity, however noble the intention, amounts to practicing a fraud on the Cuban people. Again, we do not agree. Both education and health care are already distributed largely according to communist criteria of need, though of course the quantity and quality of what is available still fall far short of satisfying the needs of a fully developed communist society. The point is that a real beginning has been made; people understand this and respond to it; it plays a part in remolding their "human nature."

Can the same kind of progress be made in the realm of material goods? Certainly. Rationing of necessaries, assuring everyone of his or her fair share, is a first small step in the communist direction, even if goods are not thereby withdrawn from mercantile circulation. And in the case of some goods, it may not be too long a time before they can be *freely* distributed according to need.

For example, if and when the ten-million-ton sugar goal is reached, it should be quite possible to distribute sugar to the Cuban people free. Cuban consumption is only a small part of Cuban production, and it is doubtful if the amount consumed internally would greatly increase in case of free distribution. And if plans for many other agricultural products— fruit, milk, coffee, to name only a few—materialize as hoped, not necessarily in the next two or three years but even in the next decade, they too could be added to the free list.

Fidel may sound too optimistic—that is a matter of opinion —but he is certainly neither a fool nor a deceiver.

#### THE PRIVATE SECTOR OUTSIDE AGRICULTURE

Before March 13, 1968, little information was available on

the private sector outside agriculture. It was of course known that many small enterprises in the trade and service fields had escaped the nationalization decrees of the summer and fall of 1960; but to our knowledge no studies had been made, or at any rate published, of the total number, the breakdown by types of business, how many had survived for how long, how many new private enterprises had been established, and so on. Then in a speech on March 13 at the University of Havana reviewing some of the country's more pressing problems and difficulties, Fidel spoke at length about the private sector outside agriculture, quoting the results of surveys carried out by the Communist Party in various sections of Havana. Among the points he made were the following:

• In Havana alone there were 955 privately owned bars.

• These bars and even more numerous food shops and stands acquired a large part of their supplies illegally, tended to be unsanitary, and often yielded their owners profits of 25, 50, 100 or even more pesos a day.

• The proprietors were for the most part non- or counter-revolutionaries exercising a bad influence on both their suppliers and their customers.

• Quoting from one of the surveys: "Through private grocery stores the private sector sells 77 million pesos' worth of goods, out of a total of 248,961,703." (It is not clear from the context whether these figures refer to Havana or the whole country, but in either case the suggested orders of magnitude are quite startling. Nearly a third of retail food trade in private hands! If we are right in assuming that these private grocery stores bought much of their supplies from private farmers at prices much higher than state procurement prices and then resold to the consuming public, after adding on a generous mark-up, of course, we can see that up to March 13 the role of the free market—commodity production and circulation—was in reality much greater than our discussion above would suggest.[12])

• From the Party surveys: "That owners of private businesses are exploiters becomes clear when we examine data on the utilization of employees, which is the case [i.e., that they hire employees] in 31.1 percent—almost one-third—of the businesses investigated [in Havana]."

• Again from the surveys: "Of the proprietors in towns in Havana Province, 10.2 percent have been in business less than a year and 36 percent less than eight years—that is, they went into business after the triumph of the Revolution. . . . In the survey carried out by the Municipal Administration of Metropolitan Havana, the percentage is 51.7."

Having presented these facts—and many more—Fidel proceeded to draw certain conclusions:

Gentlemen, we did not make a Revolution here to establish the right to trade! Such a revolution took place in 1789—that was the era of the bourgeois revolution—just about everybody has read about it—it was the revolution of the merchants, of the bourgeois. When will they finally understand that this is a revolution of socialists, that it is a revolution of Communists? When will they finally understand that nobody shed his blood here fighting against tyranny, against mercenaries, against bandits, in order to establish the right for somebody to make two hundred pesos selling rum, or fifty pesos selling fried eggs or omelets, while the girls who work at the state enterprises earn the modest salaries, the modest incomes, that the present development of our country's economy allows? Who gave them that right?

---

[12] See pp. 121-122. The assumption that much of the supplies came from the private farmers is borne out by a statement issued later in March by the Association of Small Farmers (ANAP) which says: "It has escaped no one that these elements [private traders] have gone into the countryside day after day offering the farmers high prices for their products and afterwards reselling them to the workers at inflated prices through 'private businesses.'" (*Granma*, March 31, 1968.)

Warnings mean nothing, reality means nothing to them. They are squeezing out the last drop. While privilege lasts, they will cling to privilege up to the last minute—and the last minute is near at hand, the last minute is near at hand! Clearly and definitely we must say that we propose to eliminate all manifestations of private trade, clearly and definitely. . . .

A whole plague of businessmen remains. We recall how the *Diario de la Marina*, which was the press organ of capitalism, spoke up and threatened that any measure whatsoever that harmed the "sacred freedom of trade" discouraged business and constituted a brake on the development of trade. Who is going to believe such a thing in this country, where all the measures that could have been taken against capitalism were adopted, and where capitalism still tries to make a comeback anywhere it can? . . .

Whoever says that capitalism is easily deterred is a liar; capitalism has to be dug out by the roots; the exploitation of man has to be dug out by the roots. *(Applause.)*

Toward the end of his speech Fidel said: "Everything should teach us more, each event should strengthen the Revolution, each new experience. And we realize that this is a time for undertaking a thorough, powerful, *revolutionary* offensive."

As foreshadowed in this speech, Fidel announced two days later in another speech at the opening of a new school at Boca de Jaruco, the "nationalization, or take-over—if you wish —of all types of private businesses left in our country." This, clearly, was the key measure in what immediately became known as the "revolutionary offensive." How really radical and far-reaching a measure it was can be understood in the light of figures published in the weekly edition of *Granma* dated April 7 (see Table 17). More than 55,000 enterprises, many employing relatives and/or outside workers, constitute an important element in the economy of a small country with

a population of only eight million.[13] Its nationalization in one
lightning stroke cannot but bring significant changes in the
structure and functioning of Cuban socialism.[14]

### Table 17
### Private Businesses Nationalized
### as of March 26, 1968

| | |
|---|---:|
| TOTAL NATIONALIZED | 55,636 |
| *Food Retailers* | *17,212* |
| Grocery stores | 11,878 |
| Butcher shops | 3,130 |
| Poultry stores | 204 |
| Fish stores | 12 |
| General merchandise stores | 370 |
| Vegetable stands | 1,545 |
| Others | 73 |
| *Industrial Products* | *2,682* |
| Dress shops | 284 |
| Shoe shops | 52 |
| Hardware stores | 57 |
| Furniture and upholstery stores | 144 |
| Electric household appliance stores | 8 |
| Cigarette and cigar counters | 244 |
| Hat shops | 37 |
| Notions shops | 1,170 |
| Jewelry stores | 207 |

[13] In his May Day speech Raúl Castro put the total number of businesses nationalized at 57,600.

[14] On the evidence of Fidel's speeches of March 13 and 15, the
only private enterprisers left outside of agriculture are owners of
trucks and taxis, number not specified. Fidel justified their omission
from the nationalization decree on two grounds: first, their work is
useful to society; and second, their status as private owners cannot
outlast their vehicles, all of which are of pre-revolutionary origin and
hence have a very limited life expectancy.

| | |
|---|---|
| Bookstores | 30 |
| Flower shops | 218 |
| Others | 231 |
| *Food and Drink* | *11,299* |
| Bars | 3,198 |
| Food vendors | 3,704 |
| Snack shops | 2,302 |
| Restaurants | 2,070 |
| Others | 25 |
| *Services* | *14,172*[a] |
| Laundry and drycleaning | 6,653 |
| Photo shops | 495 |
| Barber shops | 3,643 |
| Shoe repair shops | 1,188 |
| Lodging and boarding houses | 635 |
| Auto repair shops | 4,544 |
| Others | 3,014 |
| *Industries* | *9,603* |
| Metal | 682 |
| Lumber | 3,345 |
| Hides and leather goods | 249 |
| Construction materials | 283 |
| Plastics and rubber | 54 |
| Handicrafts | 1,598 |
| Chemical products | 28 |
| Perfumes | 25 |
| Foodstuffs | 307 |
| Tobacco | 170 |
| Textiles | 148 |
| Printing | 148 |
| Heavy industry | 331 |
| Light industry | 494 |
| Others | 1,741 |
| *Unclassified* | *668* |

[a] The items in the "Services" category add up to exactly 6,000 more than the indicated total of 14,172. This suggests that the number of "laundry and drycleaning" businesses should be 653 rather than 6,653.

Why was such a momentous step taken at this time? It seems clear that the answer is more political than economic. As pointed out above (pp. 107-109), Cuba is going through a period of extreme austerity: nearly everything is rationed and even unrationed goods are, with few exceptions, frequently unobtainable. At the same time a tremendous effort is being made to increase production, and everyone is under unceasing pressure to work harder. Under these circumstances there is a natural tendency for many people to become discouraged, to become engrossed in their private troubles, to lose their enthusiasm, to become apathetic. If in addition they see that despite the general belt-tightening some people continue to enjoy special privileges or even manage to take advantage of others' hardships, they may become cynical and lose their faith in the Revolution itself. The end of this road for Cubans is usually a decision to leave the country. We shall return to these problems in Chapter 11 below; here we need only note that the revolutionary leadership is of course aware of the existence of these tendencies and moods, especially among the people of Havana—the first part of Fidel's speech of March 13 is enough to prove that—and recognizes that, if unchecked, they could become a real threat to the success of the regime's development programs.

This was the background of the revolutionary offensive in general and of the nationalization decree in particular. With potential money demand for goods and services much larger than available supplies, private businessmen and operators could profiteer at will, reaping incomes often many times as high as those of even the best-paid workers. This could not but tend to demoralize many ordinary citizens sympathetic to the Revolution but lacking the fervor of Party militants; some among them would even be tempted to quit their jobs and join the ranks of the privileged petty bourgeoisie. That this was a very real danger and hence an important reason for the nationalization decision appears clearly in an editorial in the March 31 issue of *Granma:*

As Comrade Fidel Castro indicated, the considerable number of such private enterprises existing before the triumph of the Revolution has been augmented by numerous businesses which have sprung up only in recent years. These are the haven of a host of undesirable elements, from would-be exiles, waiting their time to leave the country, to lumpen and other antisocial individuals who look upon the people's creative work with contempt and try to use the shoulders of others as stepping-stones to soft berths for themselves.

Such establishments were nests of parasites, hotbeds of corruption, illegal trading, and counterrevolutionary conspiracy. They were openly antithetical to the principles of collective creative endeavor enunciated by our Revolution.

To get a good idea of the degree of corruption spawned by these activities, we need only cite the results of the investigation made by the Party of private businesses in Metropolitan Havana. According to this report, 27 percent of the proprietors were workers before setting themselves up in business (and the great majority of these sprang up after the triumph of the Revolution). The index for Las Villas was 33.8 percent; for the interior of Havana Province, 33.3 percent; and for Oriente, 28.8 percent. It is intolerable that a worker, whose labor may benefit the whole people, should become a potential bourgeois, a self-centered money-grubber and exploiter of his countrymen.

What these figures imply is perfectly clear: a *new* petty bourgeoisie was *growing* in the heart of the socialist economy. This phenomenon is not to be compared with the survival of an old petty bourgeoisie in either trade or agriculture. As we have already seen in our discussion of the private sector in agriculture, such an old petty bourgeoisie poses very serious problems for a socialist society, but it can be contained and gradually compressed by a variety of measures which need never provoke an open and disruptive conflict. A new petty bourgeoisie growing up in the field of commodity circulation is something else again. It is not a leftover from the past but a product of forces operating in the present. As it grows, moreover, it is bound to infiltrate additional areas of the economy, to infect more and more workers, to become an increasingly powerful ideological and political force. No serious socialist leadership could afford to stand idly by and watch this process unfold; drastic action was clearly called for.

It must not be supposed, however, that nationalization by itself is a complete solution to the problem. For the time being, to be sure, it does liquidate this new class, as well as the old non-agricultural petty bourgeoisie. But it does not affect the underlying situation and hence provides no guarantee against a repetition of the process. Much therefore depends on what measures are taken to follow up the nationalization of the private sector.

Immediately, of course, there were two problems: what to do with the former owners and employees, and what to do with their businesses.

With respect to the owners and employees, the procedure has been to screen them and assign them to an appropriate job or other status in the socialized economy. To quote a report in *Granma* of April 7:

In accordance with instructions issued by the Ministry of Labor, the personnel employed in nationalized businesses are . . . being relocated.

For example, in the province of Havana 626 persons were interviewed by the Ministry of Labor on March 24 and 25. Of this group, 153 will go into agricultural work, 16 into jobs under the Ministry of Construction, and 179 into miscellaneous sectors including production and services; 30 already had employment; 25 were retired; 130 have already requested retirement pensions;

19 are physically handicapped or otherwise unemployable; and 74 cases are being studied.

With respect to the businesses, many (including all bars) are being closed down and their assets distributed to state enterprises. Others are being incorporated into the state sector, with the problems of reorganization and management being entrusted for the most part to the Committees for the Defense of the Revolution (CDR's), mass organizations based on place of dwelling (village, block, or apartment house). To quote again from the same report in *Granma:*

At this moment, in every province, comrades are being selected to serve as people's administrators of the nationalized establishments.

These administrators are being chosen mainly from the ranks of the CDR's. Many will be the same persons who acted as temporary administrators in the first moments of the nationalization.

A great many of these comrades will carry on the administrative work on a voluntary basis, since the CDR's number among their members many retired workers living on pensions who are capable of administering small commercial establishments, maimed or crippled comrades of the Revolutionary Armed Forces who receive allotments and are able to perform such work, and revolutionary housewives whose husbands provide for the necessities of their homes, etc.

The information available to date indicates that the majority of those selected are not presently employed; most are women.

It thus appears that the government is attempting to make the nationalizations an occasion not only for a socially more rational distribution of manpower but also for drawing new people (mostly women) into the active labor force.

No matter how successful these efforts may be, however, they do not touch the conditions which gave rise to the new petty bourgeoisie in the first place—the coexistence of excess spendable money incomes and unfilled needs. As long as this situation persists—and it is likely to be a long time—the objective possibility of making money by going into business to provide goods and services for which consumers are prepared to pay high prices will also persist. And as long as there are unreformed, money-minded people around, it must be assumed that new outbreaks of private enterprise will continue to occur, legally if possible, illegally if necessary. Since the effect of the nationalizations was to close off the legal road, it is logical to conclude that from now on there will be a growing problem of an illegal private sector. Unless we misinterpret him, Fidel was implicitly conceding as much when, in his speech of March 15, he said that "it has not been necessary to detain anyone, to arrest anyone," and then added:

We don't intend to treat anyone badly or leave anyone in need. The Revolution would not be humane, would not be just, if anyone were left in need. There is no such intention. But, of course, the Revolution will be firm, and, if it has to be severe, it will be severe.

In other words, what the Revolution would like, its intentions, are one thing, and what the Revolution is obliged to do is another. And whenever the Revolution is forced to be severe, the Revolution will be severe. And we believe that there is no doubt of any kind about that.

It remains to be seen how far along the road of severity the Revolution will have to go to keep a new stratum of private enterprisers from emerging.

In the long run, of course, the hope is that the problem can really be solved—that is to say, its causes can be removed—by producing enough to satisfy the people's needs on the one hand, and by raising their socialist consciousness on the other. These are subjects which will occupy our attention in the chapters which follow.

# 8
# Incentives

In his speech at Sagua La Grande on April 9, 1968 (commemorating the tenth anniversary of the general strike of April 9, 1958), Fidel said:

Many workers were accustomed to working under a boss's whip, accustomed to being able to work only a few months, plagued by unemployment, surrounded by hundreds of thousands of unemployed who were waiting for a job. When the Revolution triumphed, those workers acquired permanent work, job security, and were no longer beset by the myriad problems that had weighed on them—the likelihood of a child dying if he became sick, the need to pay for everything, the constant threat of unemployment. All those circumstances disappeared, and many who could not understand what the Revolution was all about began to work less than they had before, began to work seven, six, five, four hours a day. The tendency in the early days of the Revolution was for efforts not to increase but to fall off.

Things are better now, but the same basic problem still remains. In the 1967 report entitled *Industrial Development in Cuba*, cited above on p. 106, we read:

One cannot say . . . that manpower is totally utilized in agriculture, since investigations demonstrate that in most agricultural work the time spent working does not usually reach eight hours. This is due to defects in the organization of the work, to the inadequate functioning of production norms already established, and to the circumstances, which appear also in the case of agricultural workers, that steady work and incomes much higher than those before the Revolution, accompanied by a shortage of certain industrial products whose purchase would be an additional stimulus, make it possible for the agricultural worker to reduce his work day in some of the most difficult tasks and to maintain, nevertheless, a level of income and a way of life that represent a leap forward with respect to the previous period.[1]

We did not succeed in locating any of the investigations of agricultural labor referred to in this passage and so are unable to present data on hours worked by various groups of agricultural workers. Some idea of what the studies reveal, however, may be gathered from a report in *Granma* of August 4, 1968, on a speech by Minister of Labor Jorge Risquet after a tour of inspection in the province of Camagüey. Since Camagüey is one of the country's most important agricultural provinces and also the most thinly populated province, Risquet explained, it requires a great deal of help from the rest of the country. At this point the report continues:

"But this," he pointed out, "does not alter another fact: that if we recruit all the able-bodied men in the rural tasks of the province and manage to maintain an excellent attendance record —eight hours of every day, twenty-four days in each month— with a high average production in relation to goals, the present production of our labor force will be doubled."

This suggests that on the average agricultural workers in Camagüey are working not much more than half as much as

---

[1] *Op cit.*, pp. 32-33.

they could without undue strain or damage to their health. That this is the right order of magnitude not only for Camagüey but for the country as a whole was borne out by discussions we had with well-informed (Cuban and foreign) observers of the agricultural scene. An average work day of four or five hours was frequently mentioned, and it was generally agreed that absenteeism is a significant problem. Our conclusion was that in Cuba today the agricultural labor force is utilized at somewhere around 50 percent of practicable capacity. It follows that if means could be found to remedy this underutilization, the shortage of agricultural labor, which is probably Cuba's single greatest problem at this stage of development, could be quickly eliminated. The result would be a great leap forward in agricultural production, a general improvement in living standards, and a lessening of social and political tensions. As one economist (non-Cuban) said to us, with pardonable exaggeration, "Cuba's problems would be solved."

But, alas, there is no instant remedy, no magic formula. The attitudes of the Cuban peasantry toward work reflect their own history and the very nature of the Revolution which they did so much to bring to power. Throughout Cuba's long colonial and semi-colonial past, the peasants were the nation's forgotten men—except during the few months of the year when they were needed to bring in the export crops on which the wealth of the country's native and foreign exploiters was based. During this period they were driven mercilessly —ten, twelve, even fourteen hours a day—to earn enough to keep from outright starvation the rest of the year. The state neglected the education of their children; the Church did not even bother to send missionaries or build chapels[2] in their

---

[2] Lowry Nelson, author of the standard work on pre-revolutionary rural Cuba, *Rural Cuba* (Minneapolis: University of Minnesota Press,

midst. Spiritually, they were treated like beasts of burden; physically, they were treated worse.

The Revolution changed all that almost overnight. The Agrarian Reform gave the renter, the sharecropper, the squatter a free title to his land: they no longer had to pay rent to a landlord, and the state reduced and finally (in 1967) abolished all their taxes. With these pressures removed they could immediately increase their own consumption. Free education for their children (and themselves if they wanted it) and free and vastly improved health services brought hitherto undreamed-of benefits and opportunities to the countryside. As for the agricultural wage earners, their wages were immediately raised whether they remained on the State Farms or moved to new jobs outside of agriculture; they were now assured of year-round employment; and the new educational and health services were available to them and their families equally with all other segments of the population.

In effecting this quantitative and qualitative transformation in the living standard of the peasantry, the Revolution was being true to its nature and its promises. But it was also and unavoidably destroying the entire system of pressures which for centuries had driven the Cuban peasantry to work. At bottom this system was based on one thing and one thing only: fear of starvation. The peasant worked as much and as hard as he could because that was the only way to get food for himself and his family. After the Revolution he could feed his family much better while working much less, and the state threw in for good measure things he might have longed for but never enjoyed. All his traditional, one might almost say inborn, reasons for working hard disappeared. Unless new reasons could be substituted, the most natural and

1950), reported that he had never seen a church outside the cities and towns.

human thing in the world was for him to stop working any harder than required to enjoy his new and much higher standard of life.

But what new reasons could the Revolution substitute for the old fear of starvation? Orthodox economists are ready with a prescription: material incentives. Set prices and wages, they say, so that whoever works harder gets more. But beyond a basic minimum for everyone, an underdeveloped country like Cuba has very little to distribute as prizes for hard work. A system of material incentives, to be effective, would therefore have to abandon the idea of a basic minimum for everyone and accept the principle that only those whose work measured up to some prescribed norm would get a subsistence income. Those falling short of this norm would get less and those exceeding it more. Such a system could doubtless be arranged so that no one would actually starve to death,[3] but all the same it would be essentially no more than a modification of the old system under which the chief incentive driving the peasants to hard work was fear of starvation. For the Cuban Revolution to adopt this course would have been sheer self-betrayal and ultimately, we have no doubt, disastrous. To its everlasting credit, the revolutionary leadership has at no time shown any disposition to commit such a folly.

If material incentives are excluded, there remain only two possibilities: (1) regimentation, involving some degree of

---

[3] A subsistence income covers more than bare physical survival. As Marx put it: "In contradistinction . . . to the case of other commodities, there enters into the determination of the value of labor power a historical and moral element. Nevertheless, in a given country, at a given period, the average quantity of the means of subsistence necessary for the laborer is practically known." *Capital* (Kerr edition), Vol. 1, p. 190.

coercion; and (2) raising social and political consciousness to the point where people work hard because they want to, the reason being that they find a positive value in work and/or that they feel a sense of responsibility to the collectivity.

(1) On the whole, the Cuban Revolution has resorted very little to regimentation, though there are doubtless elements of it in the large-scale mobilizations of voluntary labor. Not that there is any physical coercion involved in these mobilizations: what pressure is brought to bear is of a social and moral character. In the next few years, however, we believe that an increase in regimentation of a more formal sort is not only possible but likely. Indeed, there are already signs of this in the growing role of the army in the economy, bringing with it an increasing application of military concepts of organization and discipline. An example of this is the Che Guevara Trailblazers Brigade, organized along strictly military lines and with officers and at least some of the rank and file from the army, which has been heavily endowed with mechanized equipment and has been clearing huge amounts of land, extending the country's road network, and digging reservoirs and building dams. But more indicative of a trend was the mobilization carried out in Oriente Province in April, called Girón Month from the fact that the invasion at Playa Girón in 1961 took place in the month of April. This mobilization was described as follows by Armed Forces Minister Raúl Castro in his 1968 May Day speech:

This year Oriente Province celebrated Girón Month with an unprecedented mobilization. . . . The Party's Provincial Committee decided against organizing along the same lines as other years so as to utilize the Civil Defense structure and test the plans for wartime.

With this objective, a pilot plan was set up on State Farm No. 8 in Bayamo. Tractors and trucks were replaced by ox-drawn plows and wagons; the use of all fuel-burning machinery or vehicles was eliminated. *(Applause.)* At the same time, 1,236 workers from Bayamo who were not essential to production went to work on the farm, . . . while their comrades continued their usual work in the factories. Many factory workers were replaced by women; the results were excellent.

We will continue to carry out experiments of this kind throughout the country on the local level and in different farm activities until we have the most accurate idea possible of what we can produce, in case of necessity, without a drop—or with the absolute minimum—of fuel. *(Applause.)*

It was decided to extend these activities in other aspects through the whole province of Oriente. The groundwork was carefully laid by all the state civilian agencies under the leadership of the Party and with the counseling of Armed Forces officers. . . .

The goal was to achieve perfect control of all the province's resources—manpower and machinery—and their most rational use. . . .

Ninety-three thousand people were mobilized on a voluntary basis for thirty days to work in agricultural production, while the factories and workshops were manned by the same workers who will keep industry going in wartime. Both these groups of workers were organized into Civil Defense squads, platoons, companies, and battalions. . . .

When the siren sounded at 6 P.M. on April 1, 93,000 workers were gathered at preselected points, surrounded by enthusiastic crowds that had come to see them off. With clocklike precision, the workers set off for their work places, as if forming a large army, in perfectly organized truck caravans, with their routes, traffic regulators and controllers, time schedules, etc. Not a single accident took place.

This particular mobilization was evidently experimental in nature and was designed primarily to test certain procedures for use in a wartime emergency. Later in his speech, however, the Armed Forces Minister made it clear that it was also a prototype for future mobilizations throughout the island:

We feel that this type of mobilization for productive work, carried out on the basis of the Civil Defense system, its military discipline and leadership . . . should be imitated next year by no fewer than three provinces. *(Applause.)* We also feel that the gigantic battle that the entire nation will wage in 1970 to guarantee fulfillment of the ten-million-ton sugar production goal and other agricultural-livestock plans should also be carried out throughout the country on the basis of the principles applied during Girón Month. To be more specific: next year Girón Month will take place in the same way and at the same time in Oriente, Camagüey, and Las Villas. *(Applause.)* And, with more experience, in 1970, with a ten-million-ton sugar harvest, we will carry out . . . a massive training exercise in the country's six provinces with the participation of all the people. *(Applause.)*

Another indication of the semi-militarization of agricultural work is the Youth Centennial Column, projected in the spring of 1968 with an initial goal of sending fifty thousand young people to work in the fields of Camagüey. In principle the Column is made up of volunteers who sign up for three years in lieu of compulsory military service. The Column is organized along military lines, and the intention is to increase its size and scope of operations in future years. According to an editorial in *Granma* of June 23:[4]

Once our job is done this year, we will organize other detachments of the Youth Centennial Column in the other provinces. Our aim is to have 100,000 young people for next year and to participate in the great ten-million-ton sugar harvest in 1970 with

---

[4] The same editorial chides what it describes as a small minority of recruiters and organizers of the Column for not adhering to the principle of voluntary membership. No details are provided, but it is a reasonable guess that in the atmosphere surrounding the launching of the revolutionary offensive, at least some members of the Communist

this well-organized, experienced work force. One hundred thousand representatives of our youth's tradition of heroism will take up this task for the honor of the Revolution.

It would be possible to cite other signs and symptoms of the trend toward a semi-militarization of agriculture—and quite likely, though to a lesser degree, of other branches of the economy—but for present purposes it is hardly necessary. No one who has been in Cuba recently or who reads the Cuban press regularly can doubt the reality of the trend. It has its roots in the necessity to combat one of the most pernicious and at the same time intractable inheritances from the past, the absence of good work habits in a large part of the Cuban population. In the long run, of course, regimentation is not the answer to this probem: it is simply the substitution of a new form of external coercion for the old form which was the threat of starvation. In the long run the solution is to instill in the mass of the people a wholly new attitude toward work, a positive attitude which recognizes in work either a pleasurable mode of expending physical and mental energy or, to the extent that this is impossible, a duty which one owes to society and to oneself as a responsible member of society.

We shall return to this in a moment, but first one thing should be clear: it makes no sense to criticize the present tendency to paramilitary forms of labor organization in the name of abstract principles of freedom and anti-regimentation. In this matter of work the Cuban Revolution faces a life-and-death issue. Either a way is found to break out of underdevelopment and to put the country on a course of self-sustaining economic advance, or else the Revolution will

---

Party and the Young Communist League showed more zeal in rounding up "loafers" and "counterrevolutionaries" than in sticking to the letter of directives from headquarters.

sooner or later degenerate and the old system of capitalist underdevelopment will be restored. And in order to break out of underdevelopment, nothing is or could be more important at this stage than a fuller utilization of the available labor supply. It follows that the revolutionary leadership must take whatever measures it deems most appropriate to secure this fuller utilization. Anyone who wants to criticize this or that measure should therefore be prepared to argue that it is in fact not appropriate and that some other course of action would achieve as good or better results.

(2) As to the long-run solution to the problem—the development of new attitudes toward work—what the Soviet economist Preobrazhensky wrote more than forty years ago is as true today as it was then: "The socialist incentives to labor do not drop from heaven; they have to be developed through prolonged re-education of human nature as it has been shaped in commodity economy, re-education in the spirit of collective relations of production."[5] The Cuban leadership is aware of this, and also of the fact that after a certain age the great majority of people are not going to change their basic attitudes and habits no matter how much re-education they may be subjected to. Hence the main hope for the future is centered on the younger generation which has come to maturity since the triumph of the Revolution. Thus, noting that "old ideas" of capitalist society had not yet disappeared, Fidel said in his speech of July 26, 1967:

The Revolution has eliminated from the minds of all the people a great many of these ideas, but it is precisely in the virgin minds of the new generation which has grown up with the Revolution that we can find fewest of these ideas of the past and can perceive most clearly revolutionary ideas. . . . So that we can affirm that

---

[5] E. Preobrazhensky, *The New Economics*, trans. B. Pearce (New York: Oxford University Press, 1965), p. 193. (The book was originally published in Russian in 1926.)

an immense mass, a mass of hundreds of thousands of young people of this country, is beginning to become accustomed and is able to work and to produce with entirely new conceptions. An enormous mass of hundreds of thousands of young people is capable of doubling and even tripling the output of traditional workers, and these young people do it not with the idea that their work is going to solve personal problems but in the belief that it will provide a definitive solution of the problems of the whole society.

Much has been done to inculcate these new incentives of service to the community. Almost every speech of Fidel and other leaders of the Revolution dwells on the theme, and all the mass communications media—newspapers, radio, TV, billboards, posters—echo the words of the leaders. Nor are these efforts confined to purely educational and propaganda activities. In what is called the School Goes to the Countryside program, school children in the cities and towns spend six weeks every semester working in agriculture, carrying on their studies at a reduced pace. One purpose of this vast program is of course purely economic—to increase the supply of agricultural labor. But its political and social aims are no less important: to accustom townsfolk to hard work with their hands, to immerse them in the practice of collective living and working without pay for the benefit of the community, to reduce the traditional gap between manual and mental labor. We visited a number of School Goes to the Countryside encampments in the Havana Green Belt (most of them are now in permanent barracks), and our impressions were wholly positive. The kids look healthy and happy, and everyone we talked with agreed that the experience was really having the intended results.

Other large-scale experiments in communist (or at least pre-communist) living and working are under way, most notably on the Isle of Pines, now also called the Isle of Youth.

Tens of thousands of young people have volunteered to go there for a period of two years. They live collectively, get most of what they need free, and work to transform the Isle into what is planned to be one of the world's leading producers of citrus fruits. We were not able to visit this project, but once again we can report a pretty general consensus among informed observers that it is going well and the young people involved are responding with enthusiasm and dedication.

It would not be correct to say that all Cuban youths are good revolutionaries or that they all react favorably to the regime's efforts to transform the people's attitudes toward work. There are dissidents, loafers, and delinquents among them,[6] and of course many who do what is expected of them without having any strong convictions or commitments. In fact one would probably be safe in guessing that while the great majority of young people are for the Revolution, the number of dedicated militants is still a minority.

As far as the future is concerned, it is much too early to attempt predictions. The remaking of human habits and attitudes is at best a slow process about which there is very little that could be called scientific knowledge. It is even hard to know whether or not solid progress is being made. All one can say with assurance is that unlike most of the other socialist countries—China of course is the great exception—Cuba is wholeheartedly committed to the proposition that "the great task of the Revolution is basically the task of forming the new man . . . . the man of a truly revolutionary conscience, the man of a truly socialist conscience, the man of a truly com-

------

[6] So far as we could discover, crime and delinquency figures are not published. Inquiries elicited the impression of experienced observers that while the incidence of crimes of violence (assault, murder, etc.) is low, the same cannot be said of theft and burglary. The extreme shortage of consumer goods of course is a continuing stimulus to crimes of this sort.

munist conscience."[7] Later in this same speech, Fidel said:

We must use political awareness to create wealth. To offer
a man more for doing more than his duty is to buy his conscience
with money. To give a man participation in more collective
wealth because he does his duty and produces more and creates
more for society is to turn political awareness into wealth.

As we said before, communism certainly cannot be established
if we do not create abundant wealth. But the way to do this, in
our opinion, is not by creating political awareness with money
or with wealth, but by creating wealth with political awareness,
and more and more wealth with more collective political awareness.

The road is not easy. The task is difficult, and many will
criticize us. They will call us petty bourgeois, idealists; they will
say we are dreamers; they will say we are bound to fail. And yet
facts will speak for us, realities will speak for us, and our people
will speak and act for us, because we know our people have the
capacity to comprehend these roads and to follow these roads.

Time alone will tell whether Fidel is right. In the meantime, it is obvious that the Revolution cannot afford to rely
exclusively on political and moral incentives. And since it has
renounced the method of material incentives, it will have to
resort to organization and discipline—what we have called the
semi-militarization of work.

How far along this road it will be necessary to go will depend on many things, perhaps the most important of which
will be the speed and extent to which the great efforts of
these last years pay off in a greater flow of consumer goods to
raise the collective level of living. If people can once be convinced that working for the community produces not only
hopes for the future but also tangible benefits for the present
in which all can share, the task of reshaping attitudes toward
work should be enormously simplified.

---

[7] Speech by Fidel at Las Villas, July 26, 1968.

# 9

# The Utilization of Resources

Under capitalism all individuals consciously and deliberately pursues their own interests, but their combined actions become the blind forces of the market which produce, aggravate, and perpetuate all the frightful evils of the capitalist system: division of humanity, on both individual and national levels, into rich exploiters and poor exploited; hunger or outright starvation for the great majority of the world's people; periodic depressions and mass unemployment; wars of repression and conquest. The Marxist critique of capitalism seeks to show how what is, for the individual, strictly rational behavior produces, for society, totally irrational consequences; to lay bare the inner workings of this process; and to demonstrate its inevitability so long as capitalism continues to exist.

The logical conclusion of the Marxist critique is that man's fate must no longer be left to the blind forces of the market, that he must overthrow the system which dooms each individual to work in isolation and put in its place a system in which the society of producers, conscious of its interests, assumes direct control over its human and material resources and plans their utilization for the achievement of humanly worthy ends. Historically, it was no part of this critique to prescribe in advance the *modus operandi* of this new society, to concoct—in Marx's phrase—recipes for the cookshops of the future. That had been the preoccupation of the utopian socialists and communists of the pre-Marxian era, and it had only served to divert attention from the central task and responsibility of socialists and communists: to wage a victorious struggle to overthrow the irrational capitalist order.

So it came to pass that the Marxist revolutionary movement had a clear idea of what it wanted to achieve—a classless egalitarian society, a society of abundance for all, a society in which everyone would be free and able to develop as a whole human being—but very little idea of how to achieve it. This is not said in criticism: reliable knowledge of the kind that was needed could only be based on actual experience, and that was lacking and could not be supplied by mere speculation. In these circumstances it is hardly surprising that revolutionaries tended to assume what was most favorable for their propaganda purposes, that the problems of running a planned socialist society would be basically simple. The big problem was taking power: after that everything would be, relatively speaking, plain sailing. Thus Lenin wrote in *State and Revolution*:

If *everyone* really takes part in the administration of the state, capitalism cannot retain its hold. In its turn, capitalism, as it develops, itself creates *prerequisites* for "everyone" *to be able* really to take part in the administration of the state. Among such prerequisites are: universal literacy, already realized in most of the advanced capitalist countries, then the "training and disciplining" of millions of workers by the huge, complex, and socialized apparatus of the post office, the railways, the big factories, large-scale commerce, banking, etc., etc.

With such *economic* prerequisites it is perfectly possible, immediately, within twenty-four hours after the overthrow of the capitalists and bureaucrats, to replace them, in the control of production and distribution, in the business of *control* of labor and products by the armed workers, by the whole people in arms. . . .

Accounting and control—these are the *chief* things necessary for the organizing and correct functioning of the *first phase* of communist society. *All* citizens are here transformed into hired employees of the state, which is made up of the armed workers. *All* citizens become employees and workers of *one* national state "syndicate." All that is required is that they should work equally, should regularly do their share of the work, and should receive equal pay. The accounting and control necessary for this have been *simplified* by capitalism to the utmost, till they have become the extraordinarily simple operations of watching, recording, and issuing receipts, within the reach of anybody who can read and write and knows the first four rules of arithmetic.

When the *majority* of the people begin everywhere to keep such accounts and maintain such control over the capitalists (now converted into employees) and over the intellectual gentry, who still retain capitalist habits, this control will really become universal, general, national; and there will be no way of getting away from it, there will be "nowhere to go."

The whole of society will have become one office and one factory; with equal work and equal pay.[1]

In writing this passage, Lenin was doubtless thinking not of backward Russia but rather of the advanced capitalist countries. Nevertheless, in the light of a half-century's experience of actual socialist planning in more than a dozen countries, it is clear that his overall vision of socialist society as one big enterprise run by simple administrative techniques was essentially beside the point. The economy is not "one office and one factory"; even in the case of a small country

---

[1] See Chapter 5.

like Cuba it is many thousands of offices and factories. And if chaos is to be avoided and desired results achieved, the activity of all these units must be coordinated by methods in which "watching, recording, and issuing receipts" can play only a very subordinate role.

Capitalism, of course, has a mechanism for accomplishing this coordination: the market. It is a complicated and subtle mechanism which grew up over a period of many centuries and which has been the subject of intensive theoretical and empirical study beginning in the seventeenth century. (It is no exaggeration to say that the heart and core of bourgeois economics is simply the theory of how this mechanism works.) The problem facing the new socialist society which was born in the Russian Revolution of 1917 was to devise a coordinating mechanism to replace the market, one which would be appropriate to the requirements and objectives of socialism to which we have alluded above.

This is not the place to review the history of how the search for a solution to this problem has been carried forward, at first in the Soviet Union and later in the other countries which broke away from capitalism after the Second World War. Suffice it to say that the Soviet Union, as it emerged from the frightful devastation of international and civil wars in the early 1920's, was too weak to attempt any great social innovations. Under the New Economic Policy, adopted at Lenin's behest in 1921, the market was allowed to play its traditional coordinating role during what was conceived of as a period of recuperation. In the countryside, where the great bulk of the population lived and worked, capitalism was soon flourishing and, if unchecked, would undoubtedly have been in a position to challenge the Bolsheviks for state power in a few years' time. It was at this juncture (1929) that Stalin initiated what has been fittingly called a second revolution, this time from the top. The *kulaks*, rural full-fledged and budding capitalists, were liquidated; agriculture was collectivized and brought under state control; and the First Five Year Plan looking to the industrialization of the country was launched.

This was the beginning of the Soviet experiment of substituting centralized bureaucratic planning for the market as the coordinating mechanism of an entire economy. Not that the market was totally superseded. Collective-farm peasants were permitted to keep private plots and to sell their produce to consumers in a relatively free market. But as far as the collective and state farms and state enterprises in other branches of the economy were concerned, they were not to make their decisions in response to the profit-and-loss indications of the market but rather in accordance with detailed directives emanating from the State Planning Board in Moscow. These directives in turn were the result of a complicated process in which local and regional economic units submitted proposals which went up to the center through the relevant chains of command, often being modified on the way, and were finally shaped and coordinated into a coherent whole by the Planning Board. The directives then went back down by the same routes, ending as mandatory action plans (covering technology, labor, and capital inputs, quantities to be produced and sold, etc.) for all the units of the socialized economy.

In terms of industrializing the country and building up its defense potential against the Nazi and Japanese threats—and these were Stalin's real aims, not the realization of the historic goals of the socialist movement—the new planning system was a tremendous success, so much so indeed that it became widely accepted that Soviet planning methods were as natural to socialism as the market is to capitalism. And when socialism spread to additional countries after the Second World War, they all, in Eastern Europe and Asia alike, adopted a planning system closely patterned after that of the USSR.

It was not long, however, before the defects of this system

of centralized planning began to come to the fore. They were essentially of two kinds, and can be roughly classified as economic and political. On the economic side the system was excessively rigid in the face of changing technologies; it turned out goods and services of poor quality; it was unresponsive to the needs of consumers; above all, it did not succeed in developing a coherent set of criteria by which to judge the rationality of resource utilization by the various units of the economy and therefore permitted the unchecked growth of waste and inefficiency. On the political side it relied on and fostered bureaucracy at every level, and it utilized material incentives to get workers to work and managers to meet and if possible exceed plan targets; and for both these reasons the system accentuated material and social inequality, created a widening gap between a privileged ruling stratum and the masses, fostered cynicism about the ideals and aims of socialism, and placed apparently insuperable obstacles in the way of an advance toward the kind of society for which revolutionary socialists had traditionally struggled.

In the light of all these shortcomings—and the list is far from complete—it became increasingly obvious, not least in the Soviet Union itself, that radical changes were indispensable.

One approach to reform, which was adopted by all the socialist countries of Eastern Europe, Yugoslavia in the lead, was to place greater reliance on the market, with its automatic disciplines and its criteria of profitability. We need not discuss this here beyond noting that it involves trying to make capitalist means serve socialist ends, and expressing our own conviction that this is a hopeless contradiction: in the long run capitalist means will create and serve their own, capitalist, ends. For the rest, except in Yugoslavia the reforms are still in an early stage, and it is too soon to pass judgment on their efficacy. One can only say that neither the example of

Yugoslavia nor the results achieved to date in the rest of the region give grounds for thinking that increased reliance on the market offers any way out of the dilemmas discussed above. Politically, on the contrary, it accentuates and multiplies the evils of the system of centralized bureaucratic planning; and it is not clear, at least at this writing, that it is yielding any large economic dividends.[2]

Another approach to the reform of the old system of centralized bureaucratic planning was to introduce greater decentralization and flexibility *without* assigning any greater role to the market. Since this involves giving greater independence and responsibility to bodies and individuals at regional and local levels, and since it does not subject them to the automatic guidelines and disciplines of the market, it follows that its success depends in large measure on the degree to which decision-makers all along the line can be trusted to use their power to achieve socially desirable ends. The adoption of this approach therefore demands that stress be put on raising the level of social consciousness of responsible workers and managers, on instilling in them a desire to serve not their own private or small-group interests but rather the interests of the people as a whole.

This second approach was the one chosen by the Chinese after they reached the conclusion, in the mid-1950's, that their original decision to copy the Soviet system had been a mistake. It accounts in large part for the continuation in

[2] On the Soviet Union, see *Soviet Economic Performance: 1966-67*, Materials Prepared for the Subcommittee on Foreign Economic Policy of the Joint Economic Committee, Congress of the United States, May, 1968. It can be assumed that the preparers of this report would have been eager to stress successes due to greater use of the market, and indeed they do express considerable optimism for the future. But the record of the first two years after the initiation of the reforms is anything but impressive.

China on the part of the leadership under Mao Tse-tung of efforts to educate the Chinese people in the classical values and goals of socialism: the various rectification campaigns of the 1950's, the socialist education drive of the early 1960's, and most recently and on far the largest scale the Great Proletarian Cultural Revolution which has been going on now for more than two years. The connection between the Chinese planning system and the Cultural Revolution is well brought out in an observation by one of the few economists from the capitalist countries to visit China recently. According to Bruce McFarlane of Australia's National University (Canberra), writing to the editor of *Scientific American:*

The disadvantage of the Chinese system is that with no free price mechanism there is no "discipline of the yuan," no check on managerial efficiency. That is why the "moral incentives" aspect has received so much emphasis during the cultural revolution. Instead of bribing managers to behave rationally (as in the Liberman scheme in the U.S.S.R.), the managers are put under pressure to have the "right" attitude toward society and are subjected to the discipline of the mass meeting.[3]

From one point of view McFarlane may well be right to call this feature of the Chinese system a "disadvantage." Most Chinese in decision-making positions were brought up in the pre-revolutionary period and can scarcely be expected to have completely overcome the un- and anti-social ways of thinking and acting which the old feudal-capitalist China engendered. No doubt they often act in ways that are not in the best interests of society. And since on many matters there are no objectively determined guidelines for them to follow, such as the market provides (or at any rate is supposed to provide), they may often not know how to act in the best interests of

---

[3] *Scientific American,* August 1968, p. 6.

society, even assuming that they have no other desire. So we may take it for granted that the Chinese system leaves plenty of room for waste and inefficiency in the utilization of resources. At the same time it must be said that as compared to the market method of reform, the Chinese system has one supreme virtue: the methods it employs are compatible with— it might be better to say indistinguishable from—the ends it seeks to achieve. For after all the real purpose of socialism is to reshape human "nature," to make "socialist man" capable of living with his fellows in a truly human collectivity. And it is precisely such a person who is best fitted to make the Chinese system run smoothly and efficiently.

Cuba joined the socialist camp abruptly and without any previous preparation, acting under the *force majeure* of U. S. economic aggression. Hardly anyone in the country had had any direct experience with economic planning, and very few had even studied the experience of other countries. It was therefore quite natural that when the revolutionary government was suddenly faced with the necessity of reorienting the country's economy and running the very large part of it which had just been nationalized, it should turn for guidance and assistance to the Soviet Union and the other Eastern European countries which had come to the rescue when the United States stopped buying Cuban sugar. The revolutionary leaders followed this course the more enthusiastically since they were understandably grateful to the Soviet Union and tended at the time to think that it was the embodiment of socialist virtue and wisdom. Later on, of course, they revised their views in this regard, but this should not cause us to lose sight of the situation which actually existed in 1960.

In practice the Soviet planning system reached Cuba via Czechoslovakia, since it was primarily Czech technicians and instructors who were responsible for guiding and advising the Cubans in their first efforts to formulate and operate an economic plan. In *The Economic Transformation of Cuba,* Edward Boorstein has given us a lively first-hand description of these initial efforts.[4] Unfortunately, no comparable account is available of Cuba's disillusionment with the Soviet system and her search, still far from ended, to develop methods of running the national economy more in keeping with Cuba's traditions and aspirations.

We know that a debate took place in Cuban economic journals in 1963 and 1964 turning around two questions of crucial importance to the nature of the planning system.[5] One of these is the degree of financial autonomy of individual enterprises, and the other is the question of material vs. moral incentives. Che Guevara was the main figure on one side, and Carlos Rafael Rodríguez, one of the leaders of the pre-revolutionary Communist Party (the Popular Socialist Party) was the best known proponent of the other view. Since it was Che's ideas which finally won out, it will be helpful to quote at some length from Mandel's summary of his position:

Cuba's nationalized industry was in large part organized in accordance with the system of trusts *(empresas consolidadas)* by branch of industry, somewhat comparable to that which had at one period served as a model for the organization of Soviet industry. The financing of these trusts came from the budget, financial control being exercised at the level of the ministries (those of Industry and Finance). The Bank played an intermediary role of secondary importance.

One of the practical objectives of the economic discussion of 1963-1964 was thus either to defend this system of organization (as was done by Comrade Guevara and those who generally supported his theses); or to replace it by a system of financial

---

[4] See especially Chapter 5, "The Introduction of Planning."

[5] See Ernest Mandel, "Le grand débat économique," *Partisans,* April-June, 1967. A partial bibliography of the debate can be constructed from Mandel's footnote references.

autonomy for enterprises, including the principle that each should strive for individual profitability. The latter thesis was defended by Carlos Rafael Rodríguez and several other participants in the debate.

The position taken by Che Guevara appeared to be rather pragmatic. He did not argue that centralized management was an ideal in itself, a model to be applied everywhere and always. He simply defended the idea that Cuban industry today could be managed most effectively in this way. The arguments advanced were essentially these: the small number of enterprises (fewer than in the single city of Moscow!); the still smaller number of qualified industrial and financial cadres; relatively well developed means of telecommunication (for the most part superior to those of other countries at roughly the same stage of development as Cuba); necessity to practice strict economy of resources and to control their utilization, etc., etc.

Most of the arguments of a general order which were advanced against this position had no relation to the factual situation as described. . . .

But some of the adversaries of Che Guevara's theses linked the question of the greater efficiency of decentralized management (and of the financial autonomy which goes with it) to that of material incentives. Enterprises which are obliged to be profitable must submit all their operations to a very strict economic calculation, and for this reason they can make much greater use of material incentives, directly interesting workers in raising the productivity of labor, improving the profitability of the enterprise (for example, through economizing on the use of raw materials), and surpassing the targets set by the plan.

In this respect again, Che Guevara's response is essentially practical. He does not in the least reject the necessity for strict economic calculation within the framework of the plan. Nor does he reject the use of material incentives. But he makes their use subject to two conditions. First, it is necessary to choose forms of material incentives which do not reduce the internal cohesion of the working class, do not set the workers against each other: that is why he advocates a system of collective rewards, for teams or enterprises, rather than a system of individual rewards. And he opposes the excessive spread of material incentives because he fears their disintegrating effect on the conscience of the masses.

He wants to avoid the whole society's being saturated with a climate of egotism and striving for individual enrichment. This concern is in the tradition of Marx and especially that of Lenin who, though aware that the use of material incentives is inevitable in the period of transition from capitalism to socialism, emphasized at the same time the danger of corruption and demoralization which would fatally result from the employment of these incentives, and appealed to the party and the masses to fight vigorously against this danger.[6]

It is apparent from this summary that Che's real concern was not maximum efficiency but rather to devise a system of economic organization which would favor instead of inhibit the development of socialist consciousness and behavior. In this, his thinking ran more or less parallel to that of the Maoist leadership in China. (This does not mean that Che was under direct Chinese influence: it would be just as logical to assume that both he and they were under the influence of Marx and Lenin.)

Before the end of 1964 Che ceased to play a personal role in the Cuban economy (in the autumn he represented Cuba at the United Nations, then went on a tour of several African countries, and finally in April, 1965, took his leave of Cuba to join revolutionary struggles elsewhere). His ideas remained, however, and the debate in which he had played so dominant a role seems to have continued behind the scenes. Some day we shall perhaps have the whole story of what happened during this period, but as of now there is very little solid information to go on. We do know, of course, that it was in these years (1963-1965) that basic changes were made in the

---

[6] *Ibid.*, pp. 26-27.

structure of economic and political institutions and that the new economic development strategy giving priority to sugar and cattle was adopted.[7] But we do not know why it was not until considerably later that Che's position in the economic debate of 1963-1964 became official government policy. Even as late as his speech to the Trade Union Congress in August, 1966, Fidel said that on a number of questions, including that of "moral stimulus or material stimulus," he had his own ideas but that he did not want to "take advantage of the influence which my position presupposes" to impose them on others. These questions, he said, would be decided by the First Party Congress which he promised within a year at the latest. Actually, no Party Congress has taken place, and Fidel did not remain so reticent for long. It is safe to say that before the end of 1966 the official line had been firmly established in favor of "moral stimulus," and that this line has played an increasingly important role in shaping all other government policies.

As far as the system of economic organization and planning is concerned, the adoption of Che's position as official policy meant the total rejection of the Soviet bloc's efforts to cure economic ills through recourse to the market. Cuba, in fact, has moved steadily *away* from the market, as evidenced by such important steps as the introduction of microplans into the private agricultural sector and the nationalization of private enterprises in commercial, industrial, and services branches of the economy.[8] Probably no other socialist country relies as little on market mechanisms as Cuba.

The system which Cuba does use is highly centralized and conforms to Che's ideas in denying financial independence to

---

[7] See Chapter 5.

[8] On microplans, see above pp. 125-128; on nationalizations, pp. 131-136.

the individual enterprises. The receipts of State Farms and of part of the enterprises in the rest of the economy go via the National Bank into the national budget which is under the direction of an office of the Central Planning Commission (JUCEPLAN). Every three months officials of the Bank meet with the directors of enterprises to discuss the sums which the Bank should turn over to them to finance their wage and investment bills, at the same time checking on the execution of the plan of production. The rest of the state enterprises outside agriculture retain their receipts and use them to pay their bills, sometimes supplementing this cash flow with credits from the Bank. Since, however, these enterprises have to channel all their profits into the national budget, the independence which they enjoy is more apparent than real: they cannot pursue an independent investment policy, nor can they use any part of their profits to reward managers or workers.[9]

All state enterprises, regardless of their financial arrangements, operate under plans which reach them from the center. In theory, the whole economy is governed by an overall plan formulated by JUCEPLAN in accordance with instructions issued by the Council of Ministers.[10] But Jacques Valier is probably closer to reality when he writes that

there is as yet no *general* plan in Cuba and no *general* model of economic development: the insufficiency of material means to

[9] On these matters see the useful article by the French economist Jacques Valier, "L'Economie cubaine: quelques problèmes essentiels de son fonctionnement," *Les Temps Modernes* (March 1968), especially pp. 1617-1618.

[10] A detailed explanation of how the plan is drawn up and how it is supposed to function is contained in a fifty-six-page printed brochure entitled "La Planificación económica en Cuba," prepared by JUCE-PLAN for a seminar "on administrative aspects of the execution of development plans" which was held in Santiago, Chile, in February, 1968 (sponsorship not indicated).

operate such a system of planning is the chief reason. There exist simply on the one hand, a certain number of plans, annual or of longer duration, prepared, according to the importance of the products, by the Central Planning Board, by the ministries, or by the enterprises themselves, and on the other hand priority allocations of resources, but without there really existing a central plan and precise coordination of the various plans among themselves. In the present state of the Cuban economy, it is felt, the positive effects stemming from the permanent mobilization of the workers—which is favored by continual changes [*déplacements continuels*] and by the frequent contacts between the masses and Fidel Castro who concerns himself *personally* with the various agricultural plans of the island—are more important than the negative effects stemming from the absence of general planning which, in any case, would be technically very difficult to put into operation at the present time.

When Valier here speaks of "insufficiency of material means," he is referring to bookkeepers and accountants and other trained personnel, all sorts of business machines (not only electronic computers), and the quality of statistical information. All of these deficiencies of course can and will be ameliorated as time goes on, and the planning system will be correspondingly improved and streamlined. In the meantime certain observations may be in order about the way the system functions in its present admittedly very imperfect state. If these observations sound more critical than laudatory, the reason is only that more is to be gained from trying to diagnose shortcomings than from celebrating successes.

In general it seems to us that waste and inefficiency in Cuba today stem not so much from technical weaknesses in the planning system, important though they undoubtedly are, as from more fundamental causes. These can be grouped under three headings: (1) certain major historically and technologically conditioned disproportions in the allocation of resources; (2) abuse of "special plans"; and (3) trying to do too much.

(1) *Major Disproportions.* As pointed out in Chapter 1, pre-revolutionary Cuba was a country of scandalous contrasts, of which perhaps the most visible and offensive was the co-existence of mass un- and under-employment of human beings along with vast stretches of good but uncleared land, at the same time that the country was importing up to a third of its foodstuffs. Elementary common sense seemed to dictate a policy of clearing the land and putting the unemployed to work with a view to meeting the people's needs from their own resources and by their own efforts. And when the revolutionary government came to power it began immediately to implement this policy. Bulldozers and tractors, already on hand and newly imported, were put to work clearing land, and they have been doing it ever since. As Fidel said in his speech of January 2, 1968, between 1958 and 1967 the area of land under cultivation increased by no less than 56 percent and it is still rising.

That this was a rational policy as long as there was a large pool of unemployed labor in the countryside seems obvious, but it is difficult to see the justification for its continuance after this labor surplus had turned into a labor shortage. To put the point in another way, if agricultural labor has already become a bottleneck—and we have had more than one occasion above to emphasize the extent to which this was true by, say, 1962 or 1963—it is surely asking for more trouble to bring additional land into cultivation. Nor does a simple look at the land/labor ratio reveal the whole extent of the damage. Land-clearing operations themselves use labor and, even more important, a good deal of valuable agricultural equipment. If this labor and equipment had been devoted to more intensive working of land already under cultivation, the result could have been increases in yields instead of the declines which have been all too common in recent Cuban experience. It might be objected that the equipment used in clearing land —bulldozers, heavy tractors, etc.—is unsuited to the work of cultivating the land. But this misses the point: this kind of equipment was imported with a view to its use in clearing land; with a different policy, other kinds of equipment suitable for cultivating land could have been imported instead.

Another major and recurring disproportion in the Cuban economy has to do with the planting and harvesting of crops. If you are making an agricultural plan, you obviously have to start with the areas to be planted to the different crops. Now, in the present state of knowledge, technology, availability of resources, etc., Cuba can plant a great deal more than it can harvest. For example, mechanization is more advanced in planting than in harvesting; and most planting takes place in the May-July months when the seasonal demand for labor is relatively low. It follows that plans which are geared to the capacity to palnt, as is the case in Cuba, are sure to run into harvesting troubles. Every year at harvest time the problem recurs: which fields and which crops should be neglected and hence sacrificed, and which should be saved? Efforts are of course made to salvage as much as possible by mobilizing volunteer labor, but this is at best only a palliative which does not touch the roots of the problem.

The losses caused by this planting/harvesting imbalance are by no means confined to the crops which go to waste in the fields. It is also necessary to take account of the fact that the resources which are devoted to raising these wasted crops could have been put to other uses. The loss is therefore a double one: the actual product of these resources (which is wasted) and their potential alternative product (which is foregone). Finally, there is a moral loss as well. Even the most conscientious managers and workers, those who work hard and do their best to carry out the plan, cannot help losing some of their enthusiasm when they see time and again that a considerable part of their effort is wasted. And in some cases the result is disillusionment and cynicism.

In diagnosing the causes of the planting/harvesting imbalance, and particularly its persistence, it needs to be emphasized that it is closely related to the previously discussed land/labor disproportion. It may even be that the policy of land clearance is the most important causal factor at work. When new lands are opened up, an irresistible pressure is generated to put them to use, which means of course planting them to crops. The tendency is therefore to gear the planting program to the clearing program and leave the harvesting problem to take care of itself—or rather leave it to the government officials and party cadres whose job is to mobilize voluntary labor.

(2) *Abuse of Special Plans.* The Cuban planning system makes provision for what are called "special plans" *(Planes Especiales).* According to JUCEPLAN, these are "organic forms of great flexibility [*agilidad*]" which

permit a favorable hierarchization of specific tasks, the direct attention of the top planning organ, and the centralization under a single direction of the handling of many concurrent problems associated with the development of productive activities in which local factors (lands, channels of communication, social-environmental aspects), technical assistance, the urgency of the tasks, etc., play a predominant role.[11]

In principle, of course, arrangements of this kind are unobjectionable. Good economic planning, like good military planning, must be flexible; and the device of special plans is an appropriate way of achieving the necessary flexibility. However, there can be too much of a good thing: too many

---

11 JUCEPLAN, *La planificación económica en Cuba,* p. 17.

and too frequent special plans can add up to no planning at all. This is not what happens in Cuba, but there is unquestionably a tendency in that direction.

There are two kinds of special plans, those which succeed in their avowed objectives and those which do not. An example of the former was the special plan for producing eggs which has already been touched on.[12] This was a tremendous success. An example of the unsuccessful special plan was the Voisin pasture scheme. We never did get a really satisfactory account of the Voisin story, but the gist of it seems to have been approximately the following: Voisin was a French agronomist who devised a certain system of rotational pastures suitable to the climatic conditions of his part of France. He was also apparently a very persuasive writer. On the Cuban side, Fidel is an avid devourer of agronomical literature, always on the lookout for new ideas and new developments which can be advantageously adopted by Cuba. He read Voisin, was enormously impressed, and invited the Frenchman to come to Cuba. Voisin was cautious about the applicability of his scheme to Cuban conditions and wanted to try it out on a pilot basis. But by this time the Cuban leadership was convinced that it had the answer, or at any rate a large part of the answer, to the crucially important problem of providing an adequate alimentary basis for the livestock program. So special plans were initiated to introduce Voisin's ideas on a nationwide scale. Before this could be done Voisin himself died of a heart attack in Cuba and was given a hero's funeral. In 1966 some 3,000 Voisin pastures were projected and begun. Communist Party cadres, who played the leading role in this drive, were obliged to devote intensive study to the works of Voisin; more than half of the total investment in agriculture that year went into

---

[12] See above, pp. 104-105.

the pastures. But the whole affair was short-lived. Under Cuban conditions the pastures did not give the results which had been hoped for: many were never completed and others were converted to other uses.[13]

The Voisin story shows in exaggerated form certain characteristics which seem to be endemic to Cuban economic practice: enthusiastic receptivity to new ideas and methods; impatience to take advantage of them, resulting in an unwillingness to go through the lengthy and often frustrating process of proving them out; readiness to gamble in a big way; absence, in the aftermath of a failure, of any serious effort at self-criticism. Some of these qualities are admirable, but unfortunately they do add up to a pattern which guarantees a lot of waste.

(3) *Trying To Do Too Much.* A revolutionary regime almost inevitably tries to do too much, for the simple reason that after centuries of capitalist neglect and exploitation there is so much to do. Up to a point, moreover, trying to do too much can have positive effects, tapping reserves of energy, initiative, and ingenuity whose very existence might otherwise never have been discovered. On the other hand, trying to do too much can also have negative effects. It is as true of a nation as it is of an individual that whoever starts out to do more than he can is likely to end up doing less than he can.

Trying to do too much can take two forms: setting excessively high targets in a particular sector or sectors, and doing the same thing more or less generally. Cuba tends to do both.

As an example of the first form, the outstanding case is the

---

[13] As a footnote we can add that when we got to Paris on the way back from Cuba we made inquiries about Voisin's standing as an agronomist in France. It appears that he was not well known and that those who are familiar with his work do not have a high opinion of it.

ten-million-ton sugar goal for 1970. (We are here talking about economics only. There were obviously important political reasons why Fidel originally set the goal; and since he knows a lot more about Cuban politics than we do, we are not arguing that he was or is wrong to pay the economic price for continuing to shoot for ten million tons. We are only saying that there *is* an economic price and that it is a high one.) In his book on Cuban agriculture, Michel Gutelman presents a detailed analysis of the implications of the ten-million-ton goal, beginning as follows:

The general line, such as it had been traced out in 1963 by the revolutionary leadership, was based on the idea, among others, that it was necessary to utilize to the maximum the existing capacities of production in the sugar sector. Implicitly it was decided that in addition to unavoidable expenses of maintenance and replacement, the only investments to be undertaken would be those enlarging the capacity of sugar mills where technical conditions were favorable plus, of course, the investments needed for new cane plantations to feed the enlarged industrial capacity. This line, which would have made possible an annual production of about 8.5 million tons of sugar, would have required the investment of some 150 million pesos in the industrial sector and nearly as much in the agricultural sector. In reality, the decision taken in 1964 to produce ten million tons in 1970 departs very significantly from this original strategy and, because of the qualitative change in the effort which it implies, upsets the data of the investment problem. The consequences of this change are numerous and affect the whole of the Cuban economy, even beyond 1970. They will be particularly important in relation to the proportions of the economy and the yield in terms of foreign exchange of the effort put forward.[14]

It appears from these figures that to go from seven million tons, which was approximately the country's sugar capacity

---

[14] Gutelman, *op. cit.*, p. 204.

in 1965, to 8.5 million tons would mean an investment of around 300 million pesos, half in the industrial sector and half in the agricultural sector. Gutelman then cites a Sugar Ministry study made in 1965 to the effect that going from seven million tons to ten million in 1970 would require no less than 1,020 million pesos. In other words, the first million and a half tons beyond seven million would call for 300 million pesos of investment, or about 200 pesos per ton of additional capacity; while the next million and a half beyond 8.5 million would call for 720 million pesos, or 480 pesos per ton of additional capacity. The rapidly diminishing return from additional investment beyond a certain point is thus clear.

Nor is this the full measure of the cost of adding that last million and a half tons. For one thing the import component of the investment rises as the amount increases, so that the net foreign exchange yield tends to decline. And for another thing the more Cuba produces beyond the amounts which the socialist countries have agreed to take plus what Cuba itself consumes (in 1970 this total will probably be around eight million tons), the more it will have to sell on the so-called world market and hence the lower the price it will get in hard currency. Finally, one must never lose sight of the fact that nearly every sector of the Cuban economy is in great need of additional investment and that the 720 million pesos required for the last million and a half tons of sugar is more than the total investment in all branches of the economy in 1963![15] Think what the yield of that amount of investment would be if, instead of being concentrated in one sector with sharply diminishing returns, it were spread out in a balanced investment program affecting the whole economy.

If Cuba succeeds in reaching the ten-million-ton goal by

---

[15] See above, p. 107.

1970—and we fervently hope it will—it will be a political victory of the greatest importance, all the more so since it will have been won at such a high economic cost.

When it comes to the general tendency to set excessively high targets, it might seem that no great harm is done: 80 percent plan fulfillment sounds less impressive than 100 percent, but if the target is 20 percent higher the difference, it might be thought, is only apparent. Actually this is not the way it works. Preparations and efforts are made to reach the higher established target, and it is only in the process that the impossibility is discovered. By this time things have been done which would not have been done had the target been realistic; hastily improvised corrections have to be made which may lead to the need for more corrections; material losses are incurred; and the confidence of managers and workers in the planning system, and hence also their morale, is undermined. The young French economist Isy Joshua, who worked in Cuba in the years 1963-1967, has given us the following account of how these problems occur and reproduce themselves:

We have seen how the annual state agricultural plan in Cuba presents a clear tendency to unrealism. This annual plan, often not realized, must evidently be modified in the course of execution in order to adapt itself to a changing situation. The unrealism of the initial plan is not the only reason for these modifications, far from it: unforeseen soil conditions, climatological variations, transfers of production targets from one farm to another, etc., contribute to modify the plan. Thus in the course of the year 1966 the production plan of the Artemisa *agrupación* underwent so many variations that the *agrupación* in question had to elaborate a new plan for the second half of 1966; similarly, also in 1966, the fertilizer plan of the province of Pinar del Río was changed three times. A significant fact: often when the production plan is altered other categories (supply, investment) do not evolve in a parallel way.

But sometimes these modifications are so numerous and so important that it becomes impossible each time to re-make the plan. One then has to be satisfied with elaborating "extra-plans," operative plans or additions to programmed activities. The multiplication of these operative plans, of these "'extra-plans," of these "additions," all too often brings with it the abandonment of all planning, of all programming. One is satisfied simply to conduct productive activity on a day-to-day basis. Sometimes even these intermediary steps of plan modification, extra-plans, additions are omitted: there is a direct passage from the elaboration of the plan . . . to an "operative practice" which does not necessarily correspond to any previsions.

Now, the carrying out of any economic activity necessarily assumes the solution of the decisive problem of equilibrium between targets and resources at each level. When the available resources are not sufficient to reach *all* the fixed targets (given a certain level of efficiency in the utilization of resources), the solution of the problem of targets-resources equilibrium changes to that of fixing a certain order of priorities among the various targets and of assigning the available resources to targets in accordance with these priorities. We have just seen that the annual plan which ought to be the principal instrument of prevision, direction, and control, does not resolve the decisive problem of targets-resources equilibrium at each level. . . . Each level is thus led to resolve its targets-resources equilibrium problem in its own operative practice, in accordance with an order of priorities more or less objectively determined.

This "operative practice" explains the contradictory coexistence, in the real mode of functioning of state agriculture, of anarchic decentralization on the one hand and mechanical and authoritarian centralization on the other.[16]

What happens is that when the plan is revealed as unrealistic, the lower levels impose their own solutions, but sub-

---

[16] I. Joshua, *Organisation et rapports de production dans une économie de transition (Cuba)* (Sorbonne, Paris: Centre d'Études de Planification Socialiste, 1968), pp. 64-66.

jectively and not in accordance with overall social desiderata (anarchic decentralization). The higher levels, seeing this tendency and recognizing its negative consequences, move to restore their authority and control, but once again without benefit of guidance of a plan embodying the general interests of society (authoritarian centralization). Joshua proceeds:

> Here we must point out that the two movements which have just been described (anarchic decentralization and authoritarian centralization) are not separate: they intertwine, move forward simultaneously, overlap.
>
> In a given region while resources are being centralized and concentrated on one or two activities, the other activities of the same region are in fact abandoned to initiative from below. . . . The principal activity (that is to say, considered as such at the regional level) obviously varies from one region to another. Needless to add that nothing guarantees the rationality of such orders of priority from a general social point of view.
>
> We see here that centralization realized for one or two activities, in one or two regions, necessarily means the abandonment of other activities or regions to anarchic decentralization, i.e., that anarchic decentralization perpetuates itself within the framework of the most rigid centralization, the one nourishing the other, the one transforming itself into the other. . . .
>
> It is in the context of this inadequacy of production relations that one can comprehend the laws of the appearance and development of the *"economic bureaucracy."* As we have seen, faced with anarchic decentralization, the higher levels necessarily resort to authoritarian centralization. To establish at higher levels an order of priority among goals is evidently, as we have shown, a very complicated task, especially in agriculture: these higher levels will need, in order to make decisions with a minimum of efficiency (in the sense of regulatory efficiency), a great mass of very detailed information. There will therefore be needed an important bureaucracy in the state farm (sometimes in a department of the farm), *agrupación,* province, in order to elaborate

and transmit this information; and another equally important bureaucracy at the national level to collect this information, analyze it, make calculations, make decisions, and transmit the decisions to the lower levels.[17]

The foregoing discussion of some of the major problems of the Cuban economy and Cuban economic policy—historically and technically conditioned disproportions, use and abuse of special plans, the tendency to try to do too much—may sound very critical. It is not intended to be. Nobody and no country has satisfactorily solved these problems. The vaunted efficiency of capitalism is efficiency in producing empty affluence for a small minority and hell on earth for the vast majority: mankind can no longer afford this kind of efficiency. But it is not going to be easy to find a workable and acceptable substitute. The Soviet-bloc countries, having achieved historic successes which should never be forgotten, have suffered setbacks and failures in recent years. As a result they have in effect given up the search for a viable alternative to capitalism and are now trying to find remedies for their troubles in copying capitalism. That way lies regression and ultimate relapse. Most countries in the world have still to take the first step of overthrowing capitalism, and of those which have done so only a few are struggling to find the way forward to the new society of the future. Cuba—along with China, North Vietnam, North Korea, and Albania—has the honor to be one of them. But struggling to find the way is one thing and actually finding it is another. In between lies a long period of trial and error, of experimenting and making mistakes and correcting mistakes.

In this process making mistakes is normal, and false pride should not be allowed to interfere with their being frankly discussed. What is not normal, and indeed in the long run

---

[17] *Ibid.*, pp. 73-74.

can be disastrous, is refusal to admit mistakes and hence failure to correct them.

# 10

# Technology: Hope for the Future

In the last chapter considerable stress was laid on difficulties and shortcomings in the Cuban system of resource utilization. But it would be wrong to get the problem out of focus: these are not the main reasons why Cuba is still a poor country. Nor is the fact, emphasized in Chapter 8, that the Revolution has destroyed the old capitalist system of incentives without as yet being able to replace it with a new socialist system. These are certainly important problems, and progress in solving them will undoubtedly help to improve the situation. But the heart of the matter is that Cuba, like all the other underdeveloped countries of Asia, Africa, and Latin America, operates on a low technological level. Even if all workers were motivated to work hard and their efforts were directed and guided by impeccable plans, Cuba would still be a poor country. And this will continue to be true until it masters modern science and technology and learns to apply them effectively to the solution of Cuba's specific problems.

Two quotations from recent speeches of Fidel Castro will

serve to point up the gap which exists between the present reality and what the revolutionary leadership hopes to achieve before the end of the 1970's. "In the countryside," he said on April 19, 1968, on the occasion of the commemoration of the seventh anniversary of the defeat of the CIA-backed invasion at Playa Girón, "we still find people with second- and third-grade academic levels managing State Farms, doing the best they can, and we can't ask them to do more." But the future looks very different. On September 28, Fidel said:

Thanks to the efforts of these years, there is an enormous mass of children who are studying, who will transform this country. We have figured out that in twelve years the number of inter-mediate-level technicians in our country will not be below 800,000. Some people will say, "Is everybody to become a technician?" Yes, everybody will have to become a technician, because there will not be a single activity in the future which will not require solid training. It is needed for everything—to work with fertilizers, to apply herbicides, to operate any machine. With each passing day, man will have less physical participation in production and in work. It will basically be the machines which will do the physical labor. And to control the machines, a society must be mentally prepared for it.

Cuba, then, is in the early stages of a technological revolution which will be characterized above all by the transformation of its labor force from uneducated and unskilled field hands and operatives into well-trained technicians and machine-minders. This process is well under way and has already been commented on in our discussion of the Revolution's educational programs and achievements.[1] What are the main problems to be solved and the promising opportunities to be taken advantage of?

To answer this question we must first recall what is without

---
[1] See Chapter 2.

doubt Cuba's number one dilemma: the pattern of the country's need for agricultural labor is not greatly different from what it used to be, but the Revolution has radically altered the conditions of agricultural labor supply. There is still a tremendous seasonal demand for agricultural labor in the dry months from January through April when not only sugar cane but also other major crops are harvested and (toward the end of the period) when preparation of the soil and planting of new crops takes place. But there is no longer a large pool of landless and jobless workers in the countryside which can be drawn on to meet this bulging seasonal demand for labor. Those who used to constitute this "reserve army of labor" now either have their own land or are employed on a steady basis throughout the year—on the State Farms, in construction work, in urban industry, etc. The main means by which the Revolution has tried to solve this problem has been voluntary labor in the countryside by city dwellers, but no one thinks that this is either a permanent or socially desirable solution.[2] Every one from Fidel Castro down is convinced that in the long run the only acceptable solution must be found through technology.

Paradoxically, the first advances of technology in Cuba—and this would probably be true of many other underdeveloped countries—tended to aggravate the problem of seasonal labor shortages. This is because it is much easier to mechanize the growing of crops (preparation of the soil, planting,

---

[2] The question of using voluntary labor to solve the *economic* problem of labor shortages should not be confused with the *educational* problem of combining study with work. The Cubans strongly favor combining work with study as educationally beneficial, and at present the work of students (and teachers) helps to alleviate the shortage of agricultural labor. But of course it would still be possible to implement a work-with-study educational philosophy even if there were no labor shortages.

cultivating) than their harvesting.[3] The tractors and seeders and plows and harrows needed to mechanize the growing process are relatively easy to acquire, while in the case of harvesting the necessary machines may not even have been invented yet. This particular imbalance applied with special force to Cuba because of the preponderant role of cane in her agricultural economy. "The harvesting of cane," writes Professor Kelly, "still depends heavily on hand labor, as no satisfactory machine has yet been developed to cut the cane efficiently in the field."[4] Cuba's number one technological problem was therefore a most difficult and challenging one which even the United States had not solved: to develop an efficient mechanical cane harvester.

If all cane were planted on flat land and, like corn, grew straight up to a more or less uniform height, the task of designing a mechanical harvester would be simple. One set of knives would lop off the tops and another cut the stalks just above ground level; a blower would remove the chaff; and a loader would desposit the cleaned stalks in tractor-drawn wagons, ready for transportation to the mill. But in reality cane is often planted on hilly or uneven land and much of it (particularly the heavy and hence high-yield varieties) grows every which way, forming what appear to be impenetrable tangles. The problem is therefore anything but simple.

The first attempts to develop a workable cane harvester were undertaken by Soviet designers and engineers and met with little success. Those which functioned at all were

---

[3] According to Professor Clarence F. Kelly, Director of the University of California's Agricultural Experiment Station at Berkeley: "The picking and winnowing of a crop usually accounts for at least half of the total cost of production. *It is also by far the most difficult part of the agricultural process to mechanize.*" ("Mechanical Harvesting," *Scientific American*, August 1967, p. 50; emphasis added.)

[4] *Ibid.*, p. 55.

effective only on flat land with straight-growing cane and hence had a very limited utility. We heard one estimate that in 1966 only about 3 percent of the country's cane was mechanically harvested. More recently, however, the Cubans themselves claim that they have finally solved the problem. Here is the relevant part of the article which appeared in *Granma* on April 14, 1968, announcing this momentous news:

"The test just completed on the cane-harvesting combine indicates that results are satisfactory," Major Fidel Castro, Prime Minister of the Revolutionary Government, stated at the conclusion of test runs of machinery built in Cuba for cutting and loading sugarcane carried out on Sunday, April 7, in the cane-fields of the Andrés Cuevas State Farm of the Cauto Farm Grouping in Oriente Province.

This entirely new type of cane-harvesting combine was developed by the engineers, technicians, and workers of the sugarcane division of the Ministry of Basic Industry's Center for the Development of Machinery (CDM). The work of building the combines was directed by project engineer Carlos Cruz and project planner Rogelio Rodríguez, who, after arduous work, have solved the fundamental problems—in the opinion of some experts, impossible to solve—presented by the construction of cane-harvesting equipment.

Leaders, officials, and technicians were on hand to witness the experiments with the new equipment, which did a clean job of harvesting long rows of high-yield sugarcane, of more than 120,000 *arrobas* (1 *arroba* equals 25 pounds) per *caballería* (13.4 hectares). The testing took place when the sun was well up, in fields of unburned cane as well as in fields that had been burned over. Two combine models were tested, one with rubber-tired wheels and the other with treads. Both models gave surprisingly good results.

The new Cuban combine has eliminated many of the "bugs" which plagued previous models. It has a Soviet-built chassis and motor, but the rest of the equipment is of completely new design.

The main obstacles to the use of combines to date have been the requirements of special conditions of the terrain and of the cane itself. The machines previously used did not operate well in hilly or uneven terrain, nor could they be used on tall stands of cane, since with high growth cane tends to grow close together and become entangled, the stalks reaching varying levels. This resulted in wastage, since more of the cane was cut too high above the ground, leaving long stubs, or the tops were cut off either too low or too high on the stalk.

This test has proven that the new Cuban combine works efficiently under varying conditions: on unburned cane of high yield, close together and entangled, and in fields which had been burned over. Fidel and the leaders who accompanied him on this test inspection were able to affirm that the equipment left the rootstocks of the cane intact, thus resulting in a perfectly clean cutting, flush with the ground, without tearing the cane. In addition, the tops were cut off at the right point on the stalk. The sections of cane deposited in the wagons by the combine were stripped almost clean, only a very small percentage of cane straw remaining.

This model had undergone several previous tests. The first test was made with a prototype combine in December, 1967, at Calvario, Havana Province. Major Fidel Castro was also present at the first tryout, along with Raúl Doñas, CDM Director, and project engineer Carlos Cruz. During that trial the advantages and disadvantages of the new combine were detected and modifications proposed. The Prime Minister authorized the construction of two combines for further testing; one model equipped with wheels, and the other with tractor treads. In March of this year [1968] the combines were given their preliminary trial runs in the canefields of the Rubén Martínez Villena Sugar Mill at Aguacate (Havana).

The combines were built with the idea of solving the problem of cutting and loading cane under varying conditions, filling the wagons with cane that has been stripped clean and cut into even sections. Thus the cane can be sent directly to the sugar mill for grinding. The machines were built to work in uneven terrain, for cane of varying strains, as well as for fields with varying crop yields. And, above all, the machines had to be efficient in harvesting the cane without leaving stubs on the ground and in cutting off the tops at the right point on the stalk.

The combine is equipped with a pair of lower movable blades, which cut the cane flush to the ground; an upper blade, which cuts the top off and can be adjusted to the height of the cane; and a side blade, which separates the cane stalks in one row from those in the next row and solves the problem of stalks from different rows which have gotten entangled. The stalks are stripped of straw by a strong blower system. In addition, the combine is equipped with a "terrain adapter" which raises and lowers the blades with changes in the level of the land.

This self-propelled cane-harvesting combine has a high output. It may be used for twelve hours at a time without any difficulty. Only one man is needed to operate the combine itself, with three drivers used to pull the wagons which haul away the stripped cane. The estimated output of the combine is between 25,000 and 30,000 *arrobas* a day, although the exact volume can be judged better after the combines are put to intensive work under varying conditions. The Prime Minister and his group declared themselves very much satisfied with the performance of both model combines. The work went very smoothly, and there were no breakdowns or other snags. A large number of farmers from the Cauto region witnessed the tests and showed themselves enthusiastic over this new victory for our budding machinery industry. Joel Domenech, Minister of Basic Industry, project engineer Carlos Cruz, and Comrades Doñas and Esquivel, all highly enthusiastic over the huge success registered in the experimental operation of the equipment, provided Fidel with full details of the building and operation of the Cuban combines.

Fidel checked on every aspect of the operation of both combines: the cutting of the top and lower blades, the efficiency of the stripping process, the work with entangled cane stalks, the capacity of the machine, etc. He constantly exchanged opinions with other members of the group. They all coincided in predicting a great future for these combines in mechanizing the cane harvest.

During the operational tests, Major Fidel Castro stated that a number of combines would be constructed so that there could be complete mechanization of the harvest in areas supplying one of the Havana Province sugar mills next year. He added that many more combines would be built for the 1970 sugar harvest in a new plant which will be set up in Santa Clara by the Ministry of Basic Industry and the Ministry of Construction. Special wagons for loading cane cut by the combines will be built at the Güira de Melena plant, which will be expanded. Fidel also referred to the training of operators and mechanics for the new equipment. The training schools for operators will be set up at the sugar mills where harvesting is to be mechanized first, while the mechanics will be trained right at the factory in Santa Clara.

Fidel suggested that more powerful motors be used, raising horsepower to 120, on the combines to be manufactured in the future, and that preference be given to the tractor-tread model, since it can be used efficiently on any type or condition of terrain.

Observing the combines at work on cane with a great deal of straw, Fidel commented that there is no doubt that they function efficiently even when cutting and stripping such cane—and this, moreover, on terrain which was not the easiest to work on.

He was enthusiastic about the potentialities of this equipment once perfected, and stressed that as much information as possible should be gathered on the machines in operation while testing continues, during Girón Month [April], so that this information can be used to improve the new combines which are still to be built.

When the tests were completed, Fidel expressed his satisfaction with the results. He stated that as of 1970 work will begin in earnest on the total mechanization of cane-cutting. Fidel described the Cuban combine as highly efficient and the most important achievement of our machinery industry to date.

Before we quote from Fidel's speech of April 9 in which he first commented publicly on these new combines, it should be noted that if their capacity is correctly estimated at between 25,000 and 30,000 *arrobas* a day, and if we assume that each machine requires two operators to keep it in continuous use, then the productivity of each operator would be of the order of 14,000 *arrobas* a day. This compares with the normal yield of a proficient cane-cutter of around 140 *arrobas* a day. In other words, the combine would increase the productivity of labor in cane harvesting by a factor of about 100. This may sound fantastic, but as a matter of fact it is not at all out of line with what has been achieved through the mechanization of harvesting in the advanced countries. Speaking of the grain combine, for example, Professor Kelly writes: "The usefulness of the present combine can be measured by the fact that with this machine in California the harvesting of rice (reaping, threshing, and hulling) requires less than one man-hour per acre, whereas in Japan, where the work is done largely by hand, the average labor expenditure according to a recent study is 258 man-hours per acre."[5]

Here is what Fidel said about the new combines in his speech of April 9:

The attitude of the workers and technicians of our machine industry, who, bent on finding a solution to the difficult problem of the mechanization of cane-cutting—which is one of the hardest, most arduous, most difficult jobs, one in which a man's productivity is insignificant, which requires hundreds of thousands of workers, year after year, to cut more than 30 million *arrobas* of sugarcane per day by hand, during long months, one machete blow after another—took upon their shoulders an effort started several years ago: to build a cane-harvesting machine that would solve the problem once and for all. Two of these new combines

[5] *Ibid.*, p. 52.

were field-tested only a few days ago. And they were tested not with medium-yield cane but rather with high-yield cane; not with easy-to-cut erect cane but with heavily-strawed, tangled, reclining cane.

And these machines—which are to undergo several improvements, including the replacement of their present 75-h.p. engines by at least 100-h.p. engines—performed astonishingly well: they picked up the tangled, reclining cane; cut it; removed the straw; and deposited the cane stalks into the wagon, sufficiently clean to be directly processed at the mill. *(Applause.)*

It is possible that no single thing will have a greater influence on the future of this country than these machines; it is possible that our people and our future generations will owe few debts of gratitude as great as they owe to the men who designed and built these machines. They will mean the liberation of hundreds of thousands of workers from the most backbreaking work; they will multiply our workers' productivity many times over, because it is our purpose to supply the sugar industry in the near future, year after year, with the necessary mechanical equipment.

Naturally, some of the parts for these machines will have to be acquired abroad, while others will be made here, but we aspire to have a considerable number of these machines by the year 1970.

These combines are not too demanding of the soil they work on; so long as the terrain is not hilly they cut without difficulty. And our agricultural plans contemplate the utilization of cane-growing areas close to the sugar mills to replace areas far removed from the mills.

And we have some 20 or 30 sugar mills—located in mountainous regions—where machinery cannot be used even for loading cane. Our plan is to discontinue the operation of these mills between 1970 and 1975 and to increase the capacity of mills located in flat areas—which are, in fact, the most important mills—in order to mechanize the harvesting of sugarcane one hundred percent between 1970 and 1975. *(Applause.)* Therefore we are going to produce our ten million tons of sugar in 1970 by utilizing a certain number of machines, but principally by working hard, by cutting hard; but at the end of that five-year period it will no longer be necessary to cut one single stalk of cane by hand in this country. . . . Imagine the progressive liberation of hundreds of thousands of men now working in agriculture! Imagine the mechanization of all of our agriculture!

Other tasks will remain, such as picking coffee and fruit, but these are tasks which are not arduous, tasks that can be carried out by young people, by women, by youngsters.[6]

How many men will be liberated, how much manpower will be liberated by the mechanization of our agriculture! And we can affirm with full confidence that the present pace of our development will permit our agriculture to rank among the most advanced in the world.

It is of course a long way from the testing of experimental models to the introduction of reliable machines on a mass scale, and past Cuban enthusiasm for innovations which failed to pan out should temper optimism with caution. Nevertheless, there is no doubt whatever that the problem of the mechanical harvesting of cane can and will be solved, and it is perfectly logical that Cuba, the world's largest producer of sugar from cane, should be the first to solve it. If success is now really in sight, Fidel's anticipation of the great benefits to come should be fully justified.

Cuba has another technological need which ranks in importance with the need for an efficient mechanical cane harvester, and this is the need for irrigation. The reason is partly the frequency and severity of droughts which in the past have so often played hob with Cuba's agricultural economy.[7]

---

[6] Sooner or later these crops will also be mechanized. Professor Kelly, in the article already cited, points out that in the United States rapid progress is already being made in mechanical fruit-picking; and a Republic Steel advertisement in a recent issue of *Business Week* (July 13, 1968) speaks of "berry pickers that will harvest grapes and coffee beans, too!"

[7] See above, pp. 88-92.

But there are other reasons as well. Rainfall, when it does come, is often in excessive amounts in a few days' time (this is especially true during hurricanes which are common in the summer and autumn months in the Caribbean), resulting in widespread flooding. Dams therefore serve the dual purpose of water conservation and flood control. But even more important is the fact that proper irrigation can almost completely remove the seasonal factor from Cuban agriculture. Apart from rainfall, the Cuban climate is such that crops can be grown with nearly equal facility in any season. Irrigation will therefore permit on the one hand the continuous use of land and hence the growing of multiple crops, and on the other hand the scheduling of operations so as to eliminate seasonal bulges in the demand for agricultural labor. It is hard to exaggerate the importance of this last factor. Along with the mechanical cane harvester, it will make possible a dramatic change in the labor supply situation in the countryside. A small, technically well-trained labor force fully employed the year round will be all that will be needed. In a speech inaugurating several water conservation projects in Oriente Province on May 30, Fidel put the point this way:

> . . . this whole [irrigation] program will permit a distribution of work throughout the entire year, and we will have a greatly diversified, very developed, highly modernized and mechanized agriculture, taking advantage of all the strong points of a geographic region where the sun shines all year round. If there is sun and water and fertilizer, crops will grow here all year round, and then—when man has the upper hand—our tropical climate will be changed from an obstacle in the path of man's progress into a splendid friend of man.[8]

Unlike mechanical harvesting, irrigation did not and does not call for any new inventions. But for Cuba it has meant

---

[8] *Granma,* June 9, 1968.

the necessity to build up a branch of its economy which was virtually nonexistent before the Revolution, and this has unavoidably been a slow, painful, and costly process. A recent survey published in *Granma* gives the following account of the state of the water conservation program:[9]

> Let us conserve every drop of water! This has been the guideline of an extraordinary water conservation program taking place throughout Cuba. Dams are being built from Guane in the west to Guantánamo in the east, and on the Isle of Pines as well. Thousands of workers and technicians feverishly building, building, are out to make our Prime Minister's words a reality. New projects are already in operation. Water is now being stored instead of draining off into the sea. Caonao Dam inaugurated.... The El Mate and Paso Malo dams nearing completion. . . . Retaining walls going up at the Siguaney, Río del Medío-Las Nuevas and Cristal dams.... To dam up 52,000,000 cubic meters (almost 14,000,000,000 gallons) of water from the Cuyaguateje River and 23,000,000 cubic meters (over 6,000,000,000 gallons) from the Salado River this year.... A number of dams completed in the Havana Green Belt. . . . The Ramírez and Sofía dams under construction in Pinar del Río. . . . The La Laguna Dam being built in Camagüey Province.... The Tacajó and Clotilde dams going up in Oriente Province.... A program for the construction of small-scale dams under way throughout the nation.... Two reservoirs completed for the bean-growing program at Velasco in Oriente.[10]

Each new news item concerning these projects reflects the hard —at times even heroic—work of a people in revolution, a people that is becoming more and more aware of the importance of these works for water conservation and control for the future of its country.

---

[9] "The Revolutionary Offensive at Work in Water Conservation," *Granma*, June 23, 1968.

[10] The punctuation of this paragraph is that of the original and does not indicate omissions.

At the time of the triumph of the Revolution there were just six dams completed and functioning in all of Cuba. The total capacity of these dams was not even 30,000,000 cubic meters (less than 8,000,000,000 gallons) of water. These storage dams were part of the water-supply systems for the cities of Santa Clara, Camagüey, Holguín, and Santiago de Cuba. The Hanabanilla Hydroelectric Station—with a reservoir created by the Hanabanilla and Jibacoa dams—was only half finished; it was completed by the Revolution at the end of 1962. The plans for this project were drawn up by a U.S. firm, which also directed the construction work. There was nothing else—not a single sizable reservoir for irrigating farmlands.

The nation had few technicians who knew anything about dam-building. There was not even the most elementary information concerning the volume of water in the rivers or the amount of rainfall in the river basins. There were no geologists to make studies for adequate sites. Little construction equipment was available. In fact, it was necessary to begin from scratch; to start from zero on the road to development.

Very soon after the triumph of the Revolution, work was begun on several dams. However, it was not until the National Institute of Water Resources was set up [1962] that this work moved forward at a steady pace. . . .

It often takes years to complete dams—years in which machines, materials, and hundreds of laborers are tied up in these projects. These resources, if employed in other branches of the economy, would perhaps bring in returns much sooner. However, only by making these investments will we be able to have an assured water supply. We can see this already in the reservoirs, which are now beginning to yield returns.

Looking back at the past, comparing our accomplishments with what there was in the past, comparing our present pace of work with what was being done before, we have every reason for pride. But the picture is somewhat different if we think of what is yet to be done. Even all these projects will not be nearly enough to fully protect us from drought. We have advanced tremendously, but the way is long. We must now move forward with increasing momentum. This is the meaning of the revolutionary offensive in the field of water conservation.

In his May 30 speech, Fidel said that "within five years we will be able to provide irrigation for more than 50 percent of the nation's farmlands." That would leave quite a long way to go at the end of the five-year period, so that it is probably safe to assume that irrigation work will continue through the 1970's with benefits gradually accruing as more and more projects are completed. Here, as in the case of the mechanization of the cane harvest, the outlook is favorable, but it will be a long haul and no miracles can be expected in the meantime.

We have concentrated attention on the problems of cane-harvesting and irrigation because they are in a real sense decisive for Cuba's future. If and when they are solved, the labor supply problem will also be solved and the country will at long last be in a position to realize the great dreams of agricultural and industrial diversification which have inspired the revolutionary movement since the days of José Martí. At that time Cuba's technological problems will of course be more, not less, varied and numerous than they are today. But they will also be more like those of other societies which have escaped from the miasma of underdevelopment and which hardly require to be discussed within the limited framework of this study. There are, however, two areas in which Cuba either faces or soon will face special problems and which deserve at least a brief mention.

The first is the better utilization of sugarcane. In his May 30 speech, Fidel presented an interesting statistic:

Cane is a privileged plant of the tropics which has the capacity to absorb more solar energy than any other plant on earth. Suffice it to say that one *caballería* (13.4 hectares or 33⅓ acres) of land, producing about 100,000 *arrobas* of cane—which, as you know, is not a difficult figure to obtain with irrigation, and even without irrigation in years with good rainfall, with good care and fertilization—can produce five times the nutrients contained in a *caballería* of average U.S.-produced maize.

The United States has very high maize yields, and nevertheless the food value produced per land unit of sugarcane in a year is five times that per land unit of maize.

Cuba still utilizes this highly productive plant for the most part in traditional ways. It is processed into raw and refined sugar in the country's 151 mills, mostly for export; and the by-products (molasses, bagasse, sugarcane wax) are also handled in largely traditional ways. The molasses, of which around a million and a half tons annually are produced, is either sold as such or turned into rum; and most of the bagasse (what is left of the cane after the juice has been squeezed out) is burned as fuel to power the sugar mills. Already, of course, other uses are known and to a limited extent practiced. As was noted above, for example, some 75,000 tons of sugar were converted to molasses for feeding to cattle to keep them alive during the severe drought of last winter and spring, and some paper is made from bagasse. But in the future much more will have to be done along these lines, and new uses for the sugar by-products will have to be developed.

Already a beginning has been made in the production of torula yeasts from molasses. These have a high protein content and might become an important ingredient in animal diets which generaly suffer from a scarcity of proteins (fish meal from the rapidly expanding Cuban fishing industry is another possibility in this connection). But what seems to be by far the most hopeful prospect for the near future is the use of molasses in the feeding of cattle, not on an emergency basis but as a regular and major part of their diets. Work along this line is being carried out by the Institute of Animal Science at Güines near Havana, an up-to-date installation under the direction of one of Britain's leading animal scientists, T. R. Preston, formerly of Aberdeen. Already it has been shown that excellent results can be obtained from diets containing much larger percentages of molasses and urea (as a source of nitrogen) than had previously been thought possible. The potential importance of this in helping to establish a solid alimentary base for Cuba's livestock economy is heightened by the fact that international price relations are such that cane products are cheap and meat dear. We heard rough estimates, for example, that molasses, selling at $15 to $18 a ton, could be converted into meat worth $35 a ton.

Some observers believe that in the longer run sugarcane may become the basic raw material for a whole chemical industry, just as petroleum is today. A special Institute for Research on Sugarcane Products has been established to explore this field.[11] But this is music of the future: like most underdeveloped countries, Cuba lacks the scientific tradition and establishment which would enable her to launch a complex and multi-faceted research and development program of the kind that would be required.

The other special problem with which Cuba must cope is the use of her abundant lateritic ores. So far these are exploited mainly for their nickel content in the plants at Moa and Nicaro on the north coast of Oriente Province. But they also have a very high iron content (this remains true of the ore from which the nickel has been extracted: it is piled up for future use), and will sooner or later (as already men-

---

[11] Some details are provided in *Industrial Development in Cuba,* Report Presented by the Cuban Delegation to the International Symposium on Industrial Development, 1967, pp. 41, 46-47.

tioned on p. 97) form the basis of an important iron and steel industry. President Dorticós told us that the main technological problems have already been solved—whether by Cubans or by scientists and technicians from other socialist countries he did not say—and that all that is required now is sufficient external financing. But since the necessary sums would be in the hundreds of millions of dollars and since Cuba has many more immediate and pressing demands on her all-too-scarce supply of foreign exchange, it will certainly be quite a few years before practical steps can be taken to launch such an ambitious project. In the meantime, research on the "complete use of laterites" is entrusted to the Consolidated Nickel Enterprise which runs the Moa and Nicaro plants. "These investigations," says an official document, "are extremely important because they insist on the greater yield of the nickel plants. At the same time, they can be of capital importance in securing the necessary raw materials for the iron and steel industry."[12]

---

[12] *Ibid.*, p. 43.

# 11

# Economics and Politics

Writing probably in late 1966 or early 1967, Edward Boorstein, after noting the many difficulties and problems still facing the Cuban Revolution, went on to say:

But by the end of this decade, the full benefits of socialism will begin to show themselves in Cuba. The dependence on American parts for the maintenance and repair of equipment will be far less acute. Increased output of sugar, nickel, and meat will have solved the balance-of-payments problem and begun to produce a surplus. Increased output of milk and meat, chickens and eggs, pork, and other agricultural products will have produced a big improvement in the diet. The output of shoes and clothing will be greatly increased. With a large expansion of the cement and construction industries, the building of houses will be under way on a grand scale. Fidel has said that by 1970 the rate will be 100,000 dwelling units per year—more than a fivefold increase over the 1959-1963 average. Programs of education and training will have produced many tens of thousands of technicians. This and the solution of the balance-of-payments problem will have permitted an acceleration of industrialization.

All this might take a year or two more, or a year or two less. But does this really matter except to those who get paid to score debater's points against socialism in bourgeois newspapers? In the perspective of history, the early economic difficulties of the Revolution will have covered a speck of time.[1]

If it really were a matter of "a year or two more, or a year or two less," Boorstein would doubtless be right. But it is now nearly 1969, and it is clear that the envisaged goals are for the most part still not in sight. True, dependence on American parts has been largely overcome. But the balance-of-payments problem is very far from having been solved;[2] Cubans are still living on a severely austere diet; shoes and clothing are as scarce as ever; and new housing construction is not even keeping pace with the growth of population and the wearing out of the existing stock of houses.[3]

It seems to us that a more realistic estimate of when these basic economic problems can be expected to be well on the way to solution would be some time in the second half of the decade of the 1970's. This, to be sure, is still not a long time

---

[1] Boorstein, *op. cit.*, p. 225.

[2] An indication of the state of Cuba's balance of payments can be gathered from statistics on trade between Cuba and the Soviet Union. In the seven years 1961-1967 Cuba imported from the USSR an annual average of 114.8 million rubles more than she exported to the USSR. But in 1966 the figure was 174.6 million and in 1967 it was 220 million. These deficits have presumably been covered by Soviet loans and credits. (Figures for 1961-1966 from *Vneshniaia Torgolia SSSR, Statisticheskii Sbornik, 1918-1966,* Moscow 1967, p. 69; for 1967 a news dispatch by Harry Schwartz on the financial page of the *New York Times* of July 5, 1968.)

[3] Information supplied by President Dorticós who also told us that as of March, 1968, the rate of construction was no more than 10,000 units annually.

by relevant historical standards. Quite the contrary: for any country to overcome the heritage of colonialism and under-development within two decades would be a magnificent achievement. But can it be said, in the Cuban context, that a difference not of "a year or two more," but of, say, seven or eight years more would not really matter except to the opponents of socialism?

The answer, unfortunately, is no. There is an intimate two-way link between economic and political phenomena, the precise nature of which differs from country to country and from time to time. The analysis of the impact and ramifications of economic developments cannot ignore this interrelation, nor can it avoid taking account of the specific background and conditions of a particular country.

Cuba was the last of the independent Latin American countries to throw off the Spanish yoke and the first to become a full-fledged neo-colony of the United States. Thus despite a magnificent record of struggle for independence—going back to the Ten Years' War which began just a hundred years ago (in October, 1868) and encompassing the War of Independence (1895-1898) and the abortive revolutions of 1906 and 1933-1934—Cubans had no tradition of self-government either at the national or the local levels.

The Revolution led by Fidel Castro and his July 26th Movement must be understood against this historical background. The method of guerrilla warfare, adopted by the revolutionaries after the failure of their two efforts to trigger a national uprising against the Batista dictatorship (Moncada in 1953 and the "Granma" landing in 1956), was entirely in the tradition of the armed struggles led by such national heroes as Carlos Manuel de Céspedes, Máximo Gómez, Antonio Maceo, and José Martí. But the area of guerrilla operations was restricted to sparsely populated mountainous regions of Oriente Province, so that only a very small percentage of the Cuban people had the opportunity to learn the invaluable lessons of initiative, innovation, and self-reliance which come with participation in a people's war of liberation. The revolutionary government which came to power in the early days of January, 1959, following the dramatic collapse of the Batista regime, found itself in a paternalistic relation to the Cuban people—not through choice but because of the very nature of the situation. And this historically conditioned relation has continued to exist to this day, partly no doubt because of a certain inertia which operates in the social as well as in the physical world, but perhaps even more important because any attempt to change it would certainly present formidable problems.

Cuban politicians, from the time of the founding of the Republic, had always been long on promises and short on performance. Fidel understood very well the danger this legacy from the past represented for the new revolutionary regime. Either the Revolution would quickly bring tangible benefits to the masses, or their tremendous enthusiasm at the prospect of a "new deal" would wear off and give way to the old cynicism. Hence the whirlwind of reforms which the new government promulgated and implemented in the early months of 1959: rent and price reductions, wage increases, measures to expand educational opportunities and improve health care, and above all the historic land reform of May 17. Absolutely nothing like this had ever happened in Cuba's previous history. And—ironically but how fortunately—the neglect and exploitation to which Cuba had been subjected in the past now came to the aid of the Revolution. Everywhere there were unused resources—unemployed men, uncultivated land, accumulated stocks of raw materials and finished products—which now turned into precious reserves which could be drawn upon to increase output and raise living standards.[4] As far as the popular masses were concerned (the rich of course are another story which, however, does not concern us here) the successes achieved by the Cuban Revolution in its first few years were stupendous and almost certainly without precedent in any earlier revolution. The result was the inculcation in the masses of overwhelming feelings of devotion and loyalty to the new government and its supreme leader Fidel Castro. Maurice Zeitlin, using the sophisticated techniques of American sociological research, has documented for us the amazing extent to which, by 1962, these feelings permeated the urban working class despite the fact that this class had not played an important part in the revolutionary process before 1959.[5]

It would be a mistake to assume that material gains were the only factor shaping the people's response to the revolutionary government. There was the exhilaration which came from overthrowing the domination of foreign and domestic bosses, the national pride in standing up to the United States, the gratification stemming from the fact that little Cuba had suddenly become the object of worldwide interest and attention. All these factors interacted with the upsurge of mass living standards to create a quantity and quality of popular

---

[4] After our first visit to revolutionary Cuba in March, 1960, we wrote of "something that struck us again and again during our stay in Cuba, namely, the extent to which rapid and important results could be obtained merely by eliminating some of the worst abuses and wastes of the old order. To put the point in different terms, there was a very large unused (or abused) potential in the Cuban economy and society, and this circumstance has enabled the new regime to accomplish quickly and relatively easily certain things which in less favorable conditions might have taken years." (*Cuba: Anatomy of a Revolution*, p. 95). The same point is also stressed by Boorstein in *The Economic Transformation of Cuba*, especially pp. 81-83.

[5] Maurice Zeitlin, *Revolutionary Politics and the Cuban Working Class* (Princeton: Princeton University Press, 1967).

support for the revolutionary government which has few if any historical parallels.

The revolutionary leadership might have seen in this situation an opportunity to attempt the difficult feat of bringing the people more directly into the governing process, forging institutions of popular participation and control and encouraging the masses to use them, to assume increasing responsibility, to share in the making of the great decisions which shape their lives. In practice, however, the relationship between government and people continued to be a paternalistic one, with Fidel Castro increasingly playing the crucial role of interpreting the people's needs and wants, translating them into government policy, and continuously explaining what had to be done, and what obstacles remained to be overcome.

The smooth working of this arrangement depends essentially on two conditions. The first is that the government, through Fidel, should correctly interpret the people's needs and wants. The second is that the government should not make errors or miscalculations of such a serious nature as to shake the people's confidence in their leaders. The first of these conditions has always been fulfilled. Whether the second is being fulfilled is the great question mark which hangs over the Cuban Revolution as it enters its second decade of power.

The issue here is not ordinary run-of-the-mill errors and miscalculations. The Cuban government has made plenty of these without in any way jeopardizing its relations with the people. The miscalculation in question is much more fundamental, relating as it does to the time dimension of the process of economic development. Like most great revolutionaries, Fidel has always been an optimist; and his experience of winning power only two years after he and the ten other survivors of the "Granma" landing had reached the relative safety of the mountains, must have convinced him that there is virtually no limit to what revolutionary will and energy can accomplish. And this conviction can only have been strengthened by the great successes of the first years of the Revolution to which we have already referred. Against this background it is not surprising that when Cuba was finally, in 1962-1963, forced to face the grim realities of colonial underdevelopment, Fidel and his colleagues should have overestimated the country's short-term capabilities and correspondingly underestimated the time it would take to overcome the heritage of the past and to reach the high road of self-sustained economic development.

Again and again, unrealistically high targets have been set, promises have been made which could not be kept, hopes have been raised only to be disappointed. Statements like that quoted from Edward Boorstein at the beginning of this chapter—that "by the end of this decade, the full benefits of socialism will begin to show themselves in Cuba"—were common up to a couple of years ago. And they still are, though now the schedule has been pushed back: when we were in Cuba last February and March, the year was 1970. And as 1970 approaches the chances are that the target date will recede still further.

How much longer can this go on before disillusionment and cynicism undermine the ties which bind the Cuban people to their government? If the answer is that it can go on for five or ten years, then we for our part would say that there is not much to worry about. Before the 1970's are out, perhaps well before, Cuba should be over the hump, her strategy of development vindicated, her labors and sacrifices rewarded. Then in calmer times and with tensions relaxed, people and leadership can proceed to the business of putting their mutual relations on a firmer and more lasting basis.

But one must also reckon with the possibility that things may take a different turn, that a serious deterioration in the relation between people and government may set in long before any decisive improvement in the economic situation has begun to be felt. Indeed, some observers both inside and outside of Cuba believe that signs of such deterioration are already visible and that the Cuban political barometer points to stormy weather ahead.

Much of the evidence which supports this interpretation is of a kind which it is difficult for outsiders to evaluate. Certainly one did not have to be in Havana long last winter and spring to sense a sort of malaise which went well beyond the usual complaints about shortages of consumer goods, the lack of much-needed services (particularly repairs of all kinds), and the other inconveniences and hardships of Cuban life today (for example, in large parts of Havana running water is available only two or three hours a day). There seemed to be more of a tendency to blame the government and less disposition to believe that things would soon be improving. There were jokes about the wonderful things that would happen in 1970; one heard that acquaintances one had assumed to be loyal supporters of the Revolution had decided to leave the country;[6] and militants of long standing tended to be both depressed and frustrated: they felt that everything was not going well and yet that constructive criticism would be ignored or, worse still, misconstrued as lending aid and comfort to the enemies of the Revolution.

---

[6] According to U. S. government figures, as of a year ago 370,000 Cubans had defected to the United States, and no fewer than 700,000 more were on lists of those hoping to emigrate. *Resettlement Re-Cap, A Periodic Report from Cuban Refugee Center* (Miami, Florida: Freedom Tower, September 1967), p. 1. (These reports, described as "for administrative use," are put out by the Social and Rehabilitation Service of the Department of Health, Education, and Welfare.)

The existence of moods of uneasiness and discontent was frankly admitted by Fidel in his important speech of March 13, 1968. A few quotations will show the obvious depth of his concern:

We know that there are several questions in the air; we know that many persons have been waiting for a public occasion such as this one to hear our opinions concerning these questions. It is true that in the early days of the Revolution, public opinion in the capital, which has always had the characteristic—and I say this in all frankness—of being somewhat inconsistent, required our appearing on television with a certain frequency in order to explain every kind of problem, major or insignificant. . . . Why? Because of this certain inconsistency that characterized public opinion, above all in the capital, which had its periods of optimism and pessimism, of enthusiasm and discouragement. . . . It is no longer necessary to explain something every week or every day, but it has become apparent to us that public opinion is requiring some explanations concerning certain questions. . . . Concretely, we want to refer to the circumstances of protest— yes, of protest—of a certain discontent, confusion, and dissatisfaction related to the matter of the availability of consumer goods and, fundamentally, to several concrete measures, such as the suspension during these months of the milk quota for the adult population of Havana. Some persons were apparently dissatisfied with the explanation that appeared in the press, and if some people were dissatisfied, then possibly the well-intentioned people who were dissatisfied were right. . . .

In reality, we asked ourselves what the reasons might be for that certain uneasiness, that certain uncertainty that was evident. . . . In part, they have a real basis in real difficulties, and in part they may be related to such circumstances, for example, as the international relations of our Party and Government. It is possible that the need to ration gasoline and the circumstances surrounding the Central Committee meeting in which the pseudo-revolutionary current, the microfactional elements, were severely judged, have been factors that contributed to creating a certain state of disquiet and uncertainty. And, as I said, all this together with real difficulties. . . .

We are still a people characterized by great enthusiasm and decision at decisive moments, a people capable of giving up life itself at any hour, on any day, capable of any heroism at any moment, but a people that still lacks the virtue of daily heroism, a people that still lacks the virtue of tenacity, the demonstration of this courage and heroism not only in the dramatic moments but on each and every day. That is, there is a certain tenacity and perseverance still lacking in that heroism. . . .

In the light of these facts, these circumstances, these background factors, and this certain uneasiness and heeding of rumors, I wish to go into certain things tonight. For your information, allow me to point out some of the real problems and explain what they consist of.

Fidel seems to suggest here that the main problem is the fickleness of public opinion in the capital city, and this is by no means exclusively an official view. Well-informed friends who were in Cuba at about the same time we were, and whose observations of the Havana scene largely coincided with our own, told us, after staying in the countryside much longer and studying conditions there more closely than we were able to, that they found the mood among peasants and inhabitants of small towns to be as enthusiastic as ever.

The evidence is thus inconclusive, and one might be justified in assuming that no significant change has taken place in the relation between people and government, were it not for certain actions on the part of the government itself. Among these by far the most important was the suppression of the so-called microfaction in January, 1968. This is a massive political fact which cannot be ignored. On its interpretation much depends.

A plenary meeting of the Central Committee of the Communist Party was held in Havana on January 24, 25, and 26. On the last day Fidel gave a report which began at 12:20 P.M. and lasted, with recesses, until after midnight.[7] No part of this report was made public. The documents relating to the microfaction which were published are the following:

(1) Statements of the Central Committee under the headings "Aníbal Escalante and Other Traitors to the Revolution Remanded to Revolutionary Tribunals" and "José Matar Separated from the Central Committee, Ramón Calcines Separated from the Central Committee and the Party."

(2) A report filling six newspaper pages read to the Central Committee by Major Raúl Castro, Chairman of the Revolutionary Armed Forces and State Security Commission of the Central Committee.

(3) The text of an address by Carlos Rafael Rodríguez given at the Central Committee meeting.

(4) The "Prosecutor's Speech Before the Revolutionary Tribunal Trying Aníbal Escalante and 36 Others."

It is clear from this list that the government wanted the affair to have the fullest possible publicity, and there is no doubt that during the month of February the microfaction was the most widely and intensively discussed subject in Cuba.

Since the government's case was most succinctly summed up in the first of the statements of the Central Committee listed above, we reproduce this document in full:

The Central Committee of our Party, which met January 24, 25 and 26 read a report submitted by its Armed Forces and State Security Commission concerning the activities carried out by the microfaction, analyzed the different aspects of the report and was able to prove the following facts:

---

[7] All facts and quotations are from the weekly editions of *Granma* of February 4 and 11.

*First*: That a very small group of resentful, opportunistic and long-time sectarians headed by Aníbal Escalante organized a microfaction and carried out activities against the Revolution which should be judged by the Revolutionary Tribunals.

*Second*: That those who composed this infinitesimal microfaction never addressed themselves to the regular organisms of the Party to express their points of view, but, rather, devoted themselves to proselytizing and furthering ideological divergences among certain militants of the People's Socialist Party and some opportunists who, during the epoch of sectarianism, without any revolutionary merit whatsoever, had climbed to positions in the Party and the Government.

*Third*: That among the most arresting activities of these sectarian elements the following stand out: "attacks, by means of intrigues, on the principal measures of the Revolution; the distribution of clandestine propaganda against the line of the Party; an attempt to proffer distorted orientation to several nuclei of the Party; the presenting of false, calumnious data about the plans of the Revolution to officials of foreign countries with the intent of undermining the international relations of Cuba with other governments; the taking of secret documents from the Central Committee and the Ministry of Basic Industry; and the proselytizing and furthering of ideological divergences among certain militants who came from the ranks of the People's Socialist Party. These elements also carried out other acts which should also be judged by the Revolutionary Tribunals."

Aníbal Escalante and those who supported these activities have accepted their responsibility.

The Central Committee arrived at the following conclusions:

(1) The political and criminal responsibility of these acts was made more serious by the following:

On various occasions Comrade Fidel Castro issued public warnings about the activities of the microfaction. Specifically, in his closing speech at the OLAS Conference, Fidel Castro made an analysis of the problem and concretely denounced such activities. Comrade Raúl Castro also made denunciations and issued warnings about these problems. On numerous occasions several elements of the microfaction were called in to discuss their ideas and their attitudes which were opposed to the line of the Revolution. Several comrades warned these resentful long-time sectarians personally of the danger of the path they were following. None of these warnings was taken to heart, nor were they able to stop this minuscule group from continuing its activities in opposition to the Revolution.

(2) It is important that a clear distinction be established between the conduct of the group of resentful long-time sectarians who, coming from the ranks of the People's Socialist Party, fell in with these ideological deviations and carried out the criminal activities mentioned above and the clean, selfless, revolutionary and communist conduct of the near totality of the men and women who, rising from these same ranks, have maintained in the past and maintain in the present a sincere, loyal and communist position.

Some elements of the microfaction are corrupt, immoral individuals who climbed to Government and Party positions during the period of sectarianism.

Others—only a few of them—who had maintained a revolutionary attitude in the past were beginning to show an inclination toward personal corruption.

In general, the persons under arrest cannot be considered as representatives of the revolutionary militants proceeding from the former People's Socialist Party.

(3) It is also important to point out that the individuals who committed these crimes against the Revolution do not at present hold any positions of leadership in the Party. They constitute only nine Party members and a few dozen resentful and opportunistic individuals who are unknown to the people and have nothing to do with the great tasks and plans of the Revolution.

(4) The political importance of these actions stems from the following circumstances:

The microfaction came to coincide with arguments used and positions adopted against our Revolution by Latin American pseudorevolutionaries and the United States Central Intelligence Agency.

The above conclusion was arrived at after analyzing the activities, methods and arguments employed by those elements.

The fact that their objectives were absurd and impossible to carry out, since they lacked any support from our people, does not lessen the seriousness of their action, which is both criminal and contrary to the Party.

*In the first place*, because—on principle—it is absolutely intolerable that such procedures be utilized within the Cuban Revolution.

*In the second place*, because, in terms of the particularities of a socialist state, the activities carried on by this microfaction violated—both in methods and objectives—communist legality and principles, thus brazenly conspiring against the success of the Revolution.

*Lastly*, because the arguments utilized by such elements, by coinciding with those of the pseudorevolutioniaries of Latin America and the imperialists' theses, actually situate this group within the complex of forces opposing the Revolution.

*Therefore*: The Central Committee of the Party unanimously adopted the following resolutions:

*First*: To approve in its entirety the report submitted to the Central Committee by its Armed Forces and State Security Commission on the activities carried on by this microfaction.

*Second*: To dishonorably expel the Party members involved in these crimes. These members are: Aníbal Escalante Dellundé, Octavio Fernández Boris, Emilio de Quesada Ramírez, Luciano Argüelles Botella, Orestes Valdés Pérez, Raúl Fajardo Escalona, Luis M. Rodríguez Sáenz, Lázaro Suárez Suero and Marcelino Menéndez Menéndez.

*Third*: To submit to the Revolutionary Tribunals the report on the investigations carried out by the Central Committee organizations so that they may judge these crimes in accordance with their authority and the procedures prescribed by the current law.

*Havana, January 25, 1968*
*YEAR OF THE HEROIC GUERRILLA*
*Central Committee of the Communist Party of Cuba*

The first thing to note is the emphasis the Party leadership placed upon the political unimportance of the accused: "this infinitesimal microfaction . . . this miniscule group . . . only nine Party members and a few dozen resentful and opportunistic individuals who are unknown to the people and have nothing to do with the great tasks and plans of the Revolution . . . lacked any support from our people." Was this language intended, as some unfamiliar with the Cuban situation seem to have assumed, to divert attention from a really serious plot against the regime?

No, not at all. To reason in this way is to miss the point of the affair. There was only one prominent figure among the accused, Aníbal Escalante, and he was and still is deservedly one of the most unpopular men in the country.[8] The others were, quite literally, unknowns and obviously had no popular support. Why, then, was this one unpopular individual and the obscure group around him picked out for a show trial and severe punishment?[9]

---

[8] Escalante had been one of the leaders of the pre-revolutionary Communist Party — the Popular Socialist Party (PSP) — and became organizational secretary of the Integrated Revolutionary Organization (ORI) which was established as a first step in building the new post-revolutionary Communist Party. In this position Escalante set about building up a personal machine in the well-known Stalinist tradition. He was kicked out by Fidel in March, 1962, and shipped off to the Soviet Union where he remained until allowed to return to Cuba in 1964. The move against Escalante by Fidel was enormously popular. After his return Escalante was put in charge of a state chicken farm where many of the meetings of the microfactionalists are said to have taken place.

[9] Escalante was sentenced by the Revolutionary Tribunal to fifteen years imprisonment. Of the others, eight received sentences of twelve years, eight of ten years, six of eight years, five of four years, six of three years, one of two years, and two were referred to the Attorney's Office of the Armed Forces.

The only answer that makes sense is that they were used as an example, as a warning to others. But to whom?

One hypothesis is that the warning was to the Soviet Union and the other Eastern European socialist countries that they should refrain from meddling in Cuban affairs. It is true that the microfactionalists were accused of taking their complaints to Soviet, East German, and Czech officials with the hope of influencing these countries' policies toward Cuba. However, in the detailed account of these efforts contained in Raúl Castro's report nothing that could be called more serious than indiscretion is charged against the foreign officials concerned, and Raúl interrupted his report to pay tribute to the technicians of the Soviet bloc, adding: "I personally can state that in these years thousands of Soviet officers, including advisers, specialists, and technicians of all kinds, have worked with us in the Armed Forces; and there is, really, not a single complaint that can be made about them; quite the contrary, we hold pleasant memories of them and are deeply grateful to them." A warning intended for the Soviet-bloc countries would surely have been couched in very different terms.

A second hypothesis is that the warning was to other former members of the PSP. This is *prima facie* more plausible since there is no doubt that with the deterioration of Cuban-Soviet relations in the last few years former PSP members have been looked upon—and closely watched—as potential oppositionists. There is nothing, however, in the published documents of the case to implicate other former PSPers in oppositional activity. On the contrary, every effort was made to reassure them. The Central Committee statement quoted above emphasizes the importance of making a "clear distinction" between the conduct of the microfactionalists and "the clean, selfless, revolutionary and communist conduct of the near totality of the men and women who, rising from these same [PSP] ranks, have maintained in the past and maintain in the present a sincere, loyal, and communist position." And of the three top former leaders of the PSP, in addition to Aníbal Escalante, two (Blas Roca and Lázaro Peña) are mentioned by name in the Raúl Castro report as having spurned overtures from the microfaction, while the third (Carlos Rafael Rodríguez) delivered a speech to the Central Committee castigating Escalante and his collaborators, which was published in full in *Granma*. Again, one can only say that a warning intended for other former members of the PSP would surely have been couched in very different terms.

We are thus left with only one possible conclusion, that the warning was addressed to any Cubans who might feel disposed to take positions or express views which could, rightly or wrongly, be construed as aligning them with the microfaction. And even a cursory reading of the documents leaves little doubt that this could, potentially, include anyone critical of government policies or leaders. The arguments put forward by the microfactionalists, says the Central Committee statement, "by coinciding with those of the pseudo-revolutionaries of Latin America and the imperialists' theses, actually situate this group within the complex of forces opposing the Revolution." Presumably nearly all possible criticisms of Cuba have at one time or another been advanced by the pseudo-revolutionaries (the pro-Moscow Latin American Communist Parties) or the imperialists. And if more definite specifications are wanted, it is only necessary to study the Raúl Castro report. At one point Raúl interrupted his reading to interject:

I mention this business of their criticizing and of their being against this point or that in order to further clarify things. Early this morning I made the following proposal to a group of comrades who were going over this material with me: let's look for a single thing that the Revolution has done that these people support. And really, comrades, we could not find a single one which had been able to gain the support of these citizens. That is, any measure taken by the Revolution, important or not, met with their systematic criticism.

Obviously, if the microfactionalists criticized everything, anyone who criticizes anything can be accused of sympathizing with the microfaction. We do not suggest that things have come to this pass in Cuba today, but we are suggesting that the case of the microfaction sets a precedent and lays the groundwork for wholesale suppression of criticism in Cuba at any time the leadership may, in its own discretion, decide that the interests of the Revolution demand it.

If the suppression of the microfaction had been an isolated act, one would perhaps not be justified in ascribing any great political importance to it. But in reality it was part of a pattern which has been unfolding for some time. A few years ago it was possible for a debate to take place over fundamental policy issues.[10] The tones were muted and the arguments tended to be allusive rather than direct; but there could be no mistaking the existence of genuine differences within the government itself, and at least the general nature of these differences could be understood. Nothing like this is possible today. The periodicals through which the debate was conducted have been discontinued. Even the Party's main theoretical organ, *Cuba Socialista*, which had been an important source of information and analysis, was dropped without being replaced. While we were in Cuba the Party schools—educational institutions specially designed for the needs of Party cadres—were closed along with their unofficial organ *Teoría y Práctica* which had published valuable material on Cuban and foreign affairs. One by one the channels through which other than official views could reach the public have been cut off.

---

[10] See above, pp. 163-166.

Latest press reports moreover indicate that the government's long-standing policy of allowing wide latitude to artists and writers may also be coming to an end. A report from Havana in *Le Monde* of November 5 reads in part as follows:

"There are among us camouflaged counterrevolutionaries who try to stir up in our country 'Czechoslovak problems' and problems concerning socialist realism. It is necessary to act against these elements. . . ." It is in these terms that Mr. Lisandro Otero, vice-president of the National Council of Culture, has revealed the existence of a certain malaise. His speech, delivered at the national meeting of young writers, was published on Monday by the entire Cuban press. It is no accident that this talk, which was given two weeks ago, appears in Havana on the morrow of the surprising announcement of differences between an international jury and the National Union of Cuban Writers and Artists. . . . The meeting of young writers organized in Cienfuegos by the authorities in October was certainly an initiative taken with a view to the renovation of cultural structures desired by the leaders. . . . This confrontation [over the decisions of the international jury] could be the point of departure of a "cultural offensive" aiming at a total recasting of the institutions and policy of the Cuban Revolution in this field.

Underlying all these developments, and to a large extent explaining them, is the continuing difficult economic situation. Daily life is hard, and after ten years many people are getting tired. But there is more to it than that. The revolutionary leadership has made too many optimistic predictions that failed to materialize, too many promises that could not be kept. That these predictions and promises were honestly made and reflected an underestimate of the obstacles to be overcome rather than an intent to deceive the people, is an important fact; but it does little to alter the consequences. People are not only getting tired; they are also tending to lose their faith, their confidence in the leadership's ability to keep its word. The ties that bind the masses to their paternalistic government are beginning to erode.

The leadership shows by its actions that it is aware of this situation. But it seems to reason that the erosion is as yet localized in certain geographical and social regions—principally the intellectuals and professionals and functionaries of the capital city. It apparently draws the conclusion that the first necessity is to shut these people up before they infect the rest of the population. After that, the leadership counts on a sharp economic improvement to come to the rescue. When that happens, the ties between government and people will be mended and there will no longer be a need for harsh measures such as those against the microfaction.

Perhaps it will work out that way. We hope so. But if it doesn't, if there are still quite a few years of austerity and deprivation ahead, there is a grave danger that the ties between people and government will continue to erode and that the diabolic logic of the process will lead the government deeper and deeper into the ways of repression.

There appear to be two possible ways of escape from this dilemma. The first, which would certainly be the preference of the microfactionalists and their ideological comrades in Cuba and abroad, would call for a slowdown in the pace of economic development (a lower rate of investment on the one hand, increased production and importation of consumer goods on the other), more reliance on material incentives, extended scope for commodity production (i.e., profit-oriented production for free markets), and so on. Internationally, the counterpart of this rightist economic policy would be political alignment with the USSR and the adoption of a "peaceful coexistence" foreign policy looking to the eventual re-establishment of relations with the United States. What the consequences of such a program would be is perhaps an interesting theoretical question (we happen to think that the main consequence would be the restoration of capitalism in Cuba), but not one that need concern us here. For if anything seems certain in an uncertain world, it is that Fidel Castro would never consent to a sharp turn to the right of this kind.

The other possibility would be an attempt to change the character of the relationship between the leadership and the people to the sharing of power and responsibility, in other words a turn to the left. This would certainly not be easy. Historically conditioned habits on both sides would have to be broken. And an attack on bureaucratic methods of governing going far beyond what the Cubans have yet attempted would have to be launched.

Up to now campaigns against bureaucracy in Cuba have been concerned for the most part with reducing swollen and largely unproductive office staffs inherited from the capitalist past and in some instances built up during the early years of the Revolution. This is certainly a good thing: it would be totally irrational for a socialist country, suffering from a serious labor shortage, to tolerate the kind of disguised unemployment and special privilege which are embodied in the oversized bureaucracies characteristic of the underdeveloped capitalist world. But bureaucratic rule can exist irrespective of the size of the bureaucracy: its essence is the monopolization of power by officials appointed by and answerable to those above them in the chain of command.

In this sense Cuba's governing system is clearly one of bureaucratic rule. Power is concentrated in the Communist Party, within the Party in the Central Committee, and within the Central Committee in the Maximum Leader. The structure was built from the top down: first came the leader, then the Central Committee, then the regional and local organizers, and finally the membership. Cubans sometimes argue that the method of selecting the members gives the system a democratic character. In effect, assemblies of workers in factories, offices, and farms select the hardest working, politically purest, and best behaved of their number for membership in the enterprise's Party branch. This, it is argued, ensures that the Party directly represents the people and wields power in their behalf. Actually, it doesn't work out that way. Candidates for membership proposed by the worker assemblies can be vetoed by higher Party authorities who retain all the levers of power in their hands. Under these circumstances, what the worker assemblies choose is not who shall represent them but who shall join the governing apparatus and become the bearers of its policies and directives in the local situation. There is much to be said for this system: it ensures a Party membership which is young and able, close to the workers and respected by them. But what cannot be said for it is that it constitutes an alternative to bureaucratic rule.

Whether in the conditions prevailing in Cuba today such an alternative could be found, and if so what it would look like, are questions we do not pretend to be able to answer. History suggests that despite a long tradition of opposition to bureaucratic rule in the socialist movement,[12] in practice socialist societies have all adopted it as the most available way

---

[12] Marx's essay on the Paris Commune (*The Civil War in France*) was a paean to direct democracy and an implied denunciation of bureaucratic rule. For Lenin, this was one of Marx's most important writings on the theory of the state, and to the end of his life he never changed his views on the subjects it analyzed. "If Lenin was driven by practical necessities to recognize a constantly growing concentration of authority," writes E. H. Carr, "there is no evidence that he wavered in his belief in the antidote of 'direct democracy.' But he began to understand that progress would be slower than he had at first hoped and the bogey of bureaucracy more difficult to conjure." (*A History of Soviet Russia: The Bolshevik Revolution, 1917-1923* [New York: Macmillan, 1951-1960], p. 224.)

ECONOMICS AND POLITICS 221

of coping with their initial problems, which are invariably of formidable proportions. History also suggests that bureaucratic rule, once entrenched, is extremely resistant to change. In the Soviet Union there has never even been a serious challenge to bureaucratic rule since it was firmly established under Stalin in the late 1920's and early 1930's. And Mao Tse-tung's determination that China must not repeat the Soviet experience has culminated in more than two years of nationwide upheaval, called a cultural revolution, the lasting outcome of which we may not know for a long time.

Cuba's problems are not the same as those of the Soviet Union in the 1920's or those of China in the 1960's, and Fidel Castro is neither a Stalin nor a Mao Tse-tung. Whatever happens in Cuba is therefore unlikely to be a repeat performance. But it does seem that a new historical drama is in the making in Cuba today and that its course and outcome cannot but be the anxious concern of revolutionary socialists the world over.

# MONTHLY REVIEW

## an independent socialist magazine
## edited by Paul M. Sweezy and Harry Magdoff

*Business Week:* ". . . a brand of socialism that is thorough-going and tough-minded, drastic enough to provide the sharp break with the past that many left-wingers in the underdeveloped countries see as essential. At the same time they maintain a sturdy independence of both Moscow and Peking that appeals to neutralists. And their skill in manipulating the abstruse concepts of modern economics impresses would-be intellectuals. . . . Their analysis of the troubles of capitalism is just plausible enough to be disturbing."

*Bertrand Russell:* "Your journal has been of the greatest interest to me over a period of time. I am not a Marxist by any means as I have sought to show in critiques published in several books, but I recognize the power of much of your own analysis and where I disagree I find your journal valuable and of stimulating importance. I want to thank you for your work and to tell you of my appreciation of it."

*The Wellesley Department of Economics:* " . . . the leading Marxist intellectual (not Communist) economic journal published anywhere in the world, and is on our subscription list at the College library for good reasons."

*Albert Einstein:* "Clarity about the aims and problems of socialism is of greatest significance in our age of transition. . . . I consider the founding of this magazine to be an important public service." (In his article, "Why Socialism" in Vol. I, No. 1.)

DOMESTIC: $7 for one year, $12 for two years, $5 for one-year student subscription.

FOREIGN: $8 for one year, $14 for two years, $6 for one-year student subscription. (Subscription rates subject to change.)

116 West 14th Street, New York, New York 10011

# Modern Reader Paperbacks